The Peloponnesian War

A Captivating Guide to the Ancient Greek War Between the Two Leading City-States in Ancient Greece—Athens and Sparta

Free Bonus from Captivating History (Available for a Limited time)

Hi History Lovers!

Now you have a chance to join our exclusive history list so you can get your first history ebook for free as well as discounts and a potential to get more history books for free! Simply visit the link below to join.

Captivatinghistory.com/ebook

Also, make sure to follow us on Facebook, Twitter and Youtube by searching for Captivating History.

Contents

Introduction

For good reason, the Greeks are often one of the first civilizations that comes to mind when we think of ancient history. Between their advancements in science and technology and their strong traditions in philosophy, art, literature, and architecture, Greek influence is present in almost all we do today. And, of course, we cannot forget democracy. Ancient Athens was said to be one of the first true democracies, and although not perfect, this is still one of the best forms of government in existence today.

However, not all of ancient Greek history is about diving into the depths of the human existence or perfecting the way in which city-states manage their finances and care for their people. War was also a major part of the ancient Greek way of life, dating all the way back to the famed, although possibly untrue, Trojan War which took place c. 1260-1180 BCE.

But besides this storied war, early Greek conflicts consisted mainly of small skirmishes between the many different city-states competing for the scarce resources present in Greece, Europe, Western Asia, and Northern Africa.

Yet this would all change in the 5th century BCE. The Persian invasion of Greece c. 490 BCE forced the Greeks to band together for the first time ever to defend their common homeland, and in doing this, two city-states, Athens and Sparta, became far more powerful than they had ever been before.

And while the rise of Athens and Sparta helped to make the Greeks a more prominent force in the ancient world, this also helped set the stage for what would be one of the greatest wars to ever occur: The Peloponnesian War.

This war, which lasted 27 years from 431 BCE to 404 BCE, enveloped the entire Greek world, from Syracuse on the island of Sicily to the shores of western Turkey. It ravaged the Greek population and produced great hardships, and it led to the eventual downfall of the Athenian Empire and the rise of the Spartan Empire.

But during this time of great challenge, Greek culture would once again reveal itself as one of the richest and most interesting of the time. An intellectual psyche based on morality and rationalism caused people to question the nature of war more than they ever had before, as well as the functionality and purpose of democracy, and this perspective led to tremendous achievements in both art and literature. And it's during this war that the world was introduced to one of the greatest philosophers of all time: Socrates.

So, while it's true that war should be avoided at all costs, it's also true that it's a great teacher. It shows people who they are, and it forces them to rise up in the face of great adversity. And while the Athenians did eventually fall to the Spartans, neither side won or lost. The only losers were those who lived during this tragic conflict that was defined by famine and plague, and the only winners were those who came afterward and who were able to enjoy the tremendous advancements in human culture that came from one of the most prolific conflicts of all time.

Chapter 1 – Understanding Peloponnese

As is the case when studying military history, before delving into the details surrounding battles, campaigns, and peace treaties, it's important to first understand the geography. Yet this is particularly challenging in Greek history, largely because for most of ancient Greek history, Greece was not a unified nation but rather a collection of city-states that were scattered around the Mediterranean and Aegean Seas. The most powerful of these city-states were Athens, Sparta (which at the time would have been referred to as Lacedaemon), Thebes, Syracuse, Argos, and Corinth.

The causes of this war were many, but most historians point to the pressures of trade and tribute, as well as the desire to be the dominant force within Greek culture, as the primary reasons for conflict. And when we consider the geography of ancient Greece, it's easy to see why this is the case.

Peloponnese refers to the peninsula upon which Sparta was founded. It's the part of Greece that looks like a hand. It's connected to the rest of mainland Greece at the Straits of Corinth so named for the city of Corinth, which was a strategic city at the time, something that makes sense when we consider that Corinth would have been the most important city-state in between both Athens and Sparta.

Interestingly, Athens is not in Peloponnese. It is located on mainland Greece in the region of Attica. The two maps below help to show the different regions of ancient Greece, as well as some of its most important city-states. That the series of conflicts that took place between Athens and Sparta at this time in history came to be known as the Peloponnesian War can be attributed to the fact that historians have largely considered the Athenians to be the aggressors. But there are many historians who consider the Spartans to have been the primary drivers of war, and those who follow this school of thought often refer to this period as the Attica Wars. However, these individuals represent the minority, and for the sake of consistency, the term Peloponnesian War will be used throughout this study.

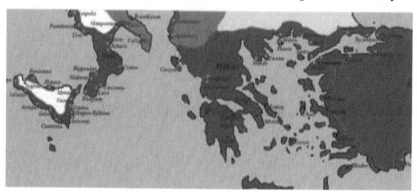

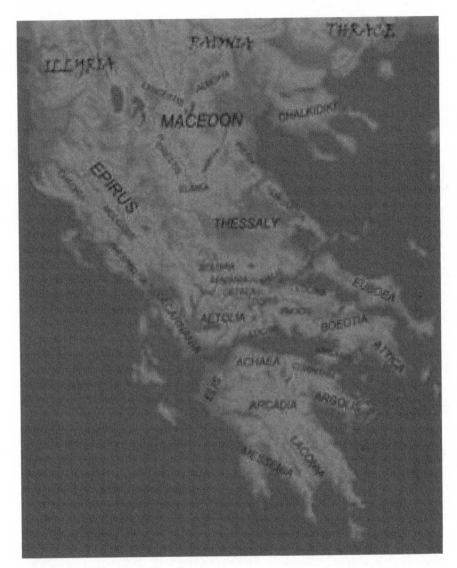

Placing Ancient Greece in Context

During ancient times, Greece would not have been referred to as Greece but rather Hellas, a name deriving from Hellen, the son of Zeus who is credited with giving birth to people, the Hellenes. It is for this reason Greek culture is sometimes referred to as Hellenic. In fact, the term Greece actually comes from Latin, and even in the modern Greek language, the term for Greece is Hellas.

This is significant because it helps set context for the Peloponnesian War which can be understood as the last major struggle among the Greek city-states for control over the Hellenes. The Hellenes likely originated in the Peloponnese; however, before the Trojan War, which took place during the 13th or 12th century BCE (this according to Greek history; modern historians debate whether or not this war actually took place), there would have been competition from other tribes and ethnicities in the region. This made the Peloponnese, like many other places in the world at the time, home to many nomadic, warring tribes.

However, over time, people began to settle in Laconia, and from there the Laconians began to drive less powerful tribes off of the Peloponnese, a move that would have been motivated by the need to secure the fertile land of the Peloponnese.

These migrations sent the Hellenes over the Straits of Corinth into Attica, where Athens is located. But Attica does not have much arable land, meaning that the region's swelling population could not be sustained. Soon, thanks to the shipbuilding of the Corinthians, the Greeks, or at this point the Hellenes, took to the sea and began settling the different islands and territories in and around the Aegean Sea, which at the time would have been called the Hellenic Sea. This put Greek colonies and city-states all throughout the Aegean and also into Asia Minor, the region that describes what is now the modern-day nation of Turkey.

All of this meant that the Greek people and the Greek culture were significantly spread out all over the Mediterranean. Greek colonies are found on the southern coast of what is now France, as well as on the now-Italian island of Sicily. And it is because of this relative decentralization that we end up with the Peloponnesian War. Athens and Sparta were able to become powerful in very distinct ways, but they both relied on the military support of surrounding city-states, as well as trade and commerce, for their own prosperity.

Because of this, the interests of Athens and Sparta began to overlap over time, and this meant that they put themselves in direct competition with one another. They came together just once to ward off an invasion from the Persians and protect their Greek homeland. But other than this, Athens and Sparta were mortal enemies who would fight on multiple occasions throughout history, with the Peloponnesian War being the final, decisive war that would help to reshape both Greek history and also the history of the entire world.

Chapter 2 – The Peloponnesian and Delian Leagues

While the Peloponnesian War is generally understood as being fought between Athens and Sparta, things were much more complicated than that. Each of the two city-states had worked to build a powerful set of alliances with surrounding Greek city-states, and the competition that resulted from the formation of these two coalitions was the source of conflict and eventual war.

The set of alliances formed by Athens became known as the Delian League which takes its name from the island of Delos, the location of the League's treasury, and also the place where the leaders of participating city-states would meet. And although the term Delian League might make things seem otherwise, the Athenians were very much the leaders of this organization. In fact, many historians prefer to use the term Athenian Empire instead of Delian League as this paints a better picture of the power dynamics within the coalition.

The Spartans led the Peloponnesian League which consisted of city-states largely in the Peloponnese, hence the name. The Peloponnesian League emerged before the Delian League, but it began to take on a new form after Athens took a more central role in the management of the Delian League, which effectively turned it into an Athenian Empire. It served as a response to the rising power and expanding ambition of the Delian League, but it soon became a force of its own that would play a large role in determining the direction of Greek history and culture.

Overall, understanding how, when, and why each of these leagues emerged is paramount to studying the Peloponnesian War. And spending the time to learn about these coalitions helps shed light on the tensions of the time, and it also helps to better comprehend why the war played out and ended the way it did.

The Greco-Persian Wars and the "Allies"

If one is to understand Ancient Greek history and the Peloponnesian War, it's important to understand the relationship between the Greeks and the dominant force in Western Asia at the time, Persia. Persian aggression against the Greeks gave the need for an alliance between the many different Greek city-states, as the only chance they had to ward off invasion was by banding together. And it was this needed coalition that gave birth to the Delian League and the Athenian Empire, both of which helped set the stage for the Peloponnesian War.

As mentioned earlier, the Greeks, specifically the Athenians, so as to accommodate their swelling population, were forced to set sail across the Aegean to settle its various islands and also Asia Minor, the region that is modern Turkey. To the Greeks, this region was known as Ionia.

However, as is the case in much of the ancient world, the Greeks were not the only ones who wanted to occupy this particular territory. Asia Minor had been the focus of many empires throughout history, such as the Assyrians, the Lydians, and, of course, the Persians.

By 546 BCE, the Persians had managed to secure control over most of Asia Minor. However, due to cultural differences and inefficiencies in the Persian government, the Persian kings struggled to maintain control over the city-states they had conquered throughout Asia Minor. In the end, they settled on establishing and empowering tyrants to rule the Greek city-states with an iron fist, but this did not play well with the more democratically-minded Greeks.

Because of the Persian failure to maintain firm control, the region was ripe for revolt, which is exactly what happened. In 499 BCE, the ruler of the city-state Miletus, Aristagoras, decided to rebel against Persian rule, and several other rulers across Ionia followed suit, putting the region in open rebellion. This period of time is now referred to as the Ionian Revolt, and it is considered to be the catalyst for the Greco-Persian Wars which would last some fifty years and essentially set the stage for the Peloponnesian War.

Aristagoras used his common Greek heritage to lure Athens and Eretria into the war and to support the Ionians who were revolting against Persian rule. However, their direct involvement was limited, with these two major Greek city-states only participating in one campaign season (498 BCE). But this effort contributed to the fall and burning of Sardis, the Persian capital in Asia Minor.

But despite this success, the Ionian Revolt was doomed to fail. The Persian king at the time, Darius the Great, sent his powerful Persian army to Asia Minor to systematically crush the various rebellions in the region and reestablish his dominance. However, Darius the Great was aware that this would likely not be the end to attempts to rebel against the Persian crown, and he saw it prudent to continue his advance into mainland Greece so as to punish the powerful city-states of Athens and Eretria for aiding their fellow Greeks in Ionia. The idea was that Darius the Great's claim to power would never be secure until the Greeks were removed from the picture.

The next few decades, from c. 490 BCE to c. 470 BCE, the Greeks and the Persians engaged in the Greco-Persian Wars which produced some of the most famous battles and military leaders in history. But the consequence from these wars that's most relevant to the Peloponnesian War is the formation of alliances between Greek city-states.

The beginning of the Greco-Persian Wars did not look good for the Greeks. Darius the Great managed to come around the Thracian coast and through Macedonia and mainland Greece, conquering and destroying Eretria along the way and adding the Aegean Islands to the Persian Empire for the first time in history. However, the historic Battle of Marathon in 490 BCE was won by the Athenians, halting the Persians in their tracks and securing Greece against further Persian invasion for some time.

However, Darius the Great died in 486 BCE and his son, Xerxes I, took control of Persia. He was eager to continue on the legacy of his father and add to his own by bringing all of the Greek people under Persian control once and for all.

The army and fleet that Xerxes I managed to assemble after the death of his father is one of the more famous of the ancient world, although many historians suspect the size and glory of the Persian army were likely exaggerated by Greek historians so as to enhance the image of the Greek effort in the war.

But no matter how big the army actually was, there was no doubting its strength, and this put the entire Greek population in grave danger, so much so that many Greek city-states actually surrendered to the Persians instead of fighting, helping to make the Persian invasion that much more daunting.

Yet not all Greek city-states chose to submit, and those who decided to resist and fight the Persians became known as the "Allies." This is the first appearance in history of the coalition that would someday be known as the Delian League, although at this point it would have been considered nothing more than a loose military alliance between Greek city-states.

Most interestingly, at least in the context of the Peloponnesian War, the Athenians and the Spartans were "Allies" in the fight against the Persians. Recognizing the threat posed by Xerxes and his great armies, these two city-states would have benefited mutually from joining together. And it turned out that this was the right move. Defeats in the land battle of Thermopylae and the sea battle of Artemisium left all of Greece except for the Peloponnese in the hands of the Persians.

In an attempt to build off these victories, Xerxes I continued southward, hoping to crush the Greeks once and for all, but he was defeated at the Battle of Salamis in 480 BCE. And the following year, the "Allies" put together the largest army ever assembled in Greek history and defeated the Persians at the decisive Battle of Plataea which sent the Persians running, effectively ending the invasion threat. This battle proved to be a decisive turning point in the entire Greco-Persian Wars, and it launched a new phase of the conflict known as the Greek counterattack.

This counterattack brought the Allied Greek armies back into Thrace, besieging and reconquering the capital Sestos, and the next year, 478 BCE, the Greeks managed to take back Byzantion, the city that would one day become Constantinople and that is now Istanbul.

The Formation of the Delian League: Athens and Sparta Split

At this point in history, the precarious coalition that had been formed between Sparta and Athens began to crumble. With mainland Greece restored to the Greeks and the Persians driven away from the western coast of Asia Minor, the Spartans believed the purpose of the war with Persia had been fulfilled and therefore did not need to continue. But they went one step further, suggesting that it would be impossible to ever completely secure Asia Minor from further attack and insurrection, and that the only way to provide for the safety of the Hellenic people living in Asia Minor would be to transplant them back to mainland Greece, effectively abandoning Greece's attempts at securing territory outside of Europe.

However, this perspective was not one that was shared by the Athenians. The Greek city-states in Asia Minor had been formed as colonies of Athens, and they were in part needed to maintain Athenian power since Attica, where Athens was located in Greece, did not have the land nor resources needed to support its large population.

This marked a transition in Greek power politics. The Allied armies that had helped make Greek defense of its homeland possible had been largely under the control of Sparta and the other powerful city-states of the Peloponnese, a coalition referred to as the Peloponnesian League. This makes sense, since by the time the Spartans got involved in the war, the Persians had managed to take control over all of Greece except for the Peloponnese. However, with the Spartans seeing no reason to continue fighting the Persians, they decided to withdraw from the alliance, a move that placed Athens at the top of the alliance of Greek city-states. This would dramatically alter the course of history as it would put Athens in a unique position to exert its dominance and become a powerful empire in the region, which would eventually lead to the clashes with Sparta and the Peloponnesian League that became known as the Peloponnesian War.

Although Athens was the most powerful member of this Alliance, it was never meant to be an Athenian-dominated institution. The term "Delian" derives from the island Delos, which is where the remaining city-states interested in continuing the war decided to meet to determine the course of action moving forward. At this meeting, the Delian League was established, and according to Thucydides, the historian responsible for recounting many of the events before, during, and after the Peloponnesian War, its purpose was "to avenge the wrongs they [the Greeks] suffered by ravaging the territory of the [Persian] king." But most historians identify three main purposes of the League: 1) to prepare for future invasion; 2) seek revenge against Persia; and 3) organize a means of dividing the spoils of war.

This approach tells us that the Delian League was first and foremost a military alliance. It shows how angry the Greeks were at the Persians as a result of the invasion, and it also hints at the budding ambition of the Greeks, specifically the Athenians, to establish an empire of their own. And it was also decidedly Greek, as there were democratic tones to the League. Membership was initially voluntary, and the idea was that each member would help protect the interests and safety of other states in the League. Yet this would dissolve over time as the Athenians became more ambitious and powerful, something that would indeed contribute to the clashes that would ensue between the Spartans and Athenians.

Membership to the League required a contribution of armed forces or payment of a tax, and most city-states chose to pay the tax. By being a part of the League, each city-state agreed to have the same friends and enemies of one another, a move that helped bring the city-states more closely together.

The Growth of the League and of Athenian Power

The Delian League was meant to serve as a military alliance and a form of mutual protection, but it quickly became a vessel for Athens to grow its power and influence in the region. Part of the reason for this is that almost as soon as the League was formed several city-states tried to revolt, and Athens responded with a heavy hand, which helped to both reduce the power of other members while also expanding its own.

For example, the island of Naxos revolted in 471 BCE in response to Athens' increasingly hegemonic role in the League. Athens responded with force, and once the rebellion was crushed, Naxos was forced to turn over its fleet to the League, which meant Athens. They were also forced to tear down their walls, and they were stripped of their vote inside the League. This move effectively made Naxos a vassal to Athens and the League, which was a sign of things to come.

However, in the early years of the Delian League, it remained focused on its original purposes and intentions. The Delian League supported a rebellion against Persian rule in Egypt that broke out in 460 BCE. By this point, the Greek leader, Pericles, was ruling Athens and sat at the top of the Delian League. He sent ships and troops to Egypt, but they were largely unsuccessful. The Athenian forces suffered massive defeats and were forced to retreat, and this meant that Egypt would remain under the control of the Persians.

Fearing retaliation, Pericles decided to move the Delian League treasury to Athens in 454 BCE, which is a move widely regarded by historians as a ploy to further entrench the Athenians at the top of the Delian League. Two more battles between the Athenians and the Persians were fought in Cyrpus in 451 and 450 BCE, and the next year, 449 BCE, the Greco-Persian Wars came to an end as a result of the Peace of Callias.

Most historians look at this move of the Delian treasury to Athens as the end of the Delian League and the beginning of the Athenian Empire. With the treasury located within the city limits of Athens, the Athenian leaders had far more control over how funds were spent. In addition to moving the treasury, Athens, under the control of Pericles, did away with the contribution of armed forces as a form of League dues, insisting instead that member city-states simply send money.

The moving of the treasury certainly helped signal to the League and the rest of the world that Athens was more powerful than ever before. And Pericles began to flex his muscles as the leader of what had essentially become an empire. He stopped using funds from the League's treasury strictly for the defense of its members, which was the initial policy of the League, and instead started spending it for the aggrandizement of Athens.

For example, after moving the treasury, Pericles ordered the construction of the Parthenon at the Acropolis. And in the ancient world, nothing screams empire and power like the building of large and expensive monuments. Pericles also ordered the construction of Athens' double walls, which helped secure access to the city's port of Piraeus, and thanks to the city-state of Megara deserting the Peloponnesian League, the Athenians were able to build walls along the Isthmus of Corinth, helping to secure Athens' southwest borders. Or, to put it more clearly, it helped to provide another layer of defense against Sparta and the evermore powerful Peloponnesian League.

But while the Athenians were rising in power, so were their neighbors, specifically the Spartans, and this would eventually lead to the demise of the Delian League and the Athenian Empire. But this happened largely because of the actions of Athens itself. Athens began to support some of the Spartans' enemies such as the city-states of Aegina and Megara. Sparta responded by sending troops in Boeotia, the region where Thebes is located.

After these initial conflicts, the Delian League led by Athens and the Peloponnesian League led by Sparta entered a brief war that is sometimes called the First Peloponnesian War. The details of these conflicts will be discussed later, but this first war between Athens and Sparta was short-lived, and a peace treaty was signed in 446/445 BCE that was set to establish peaceful relations between the two major city-states for the next thirty years. But it would just barely last half that amount of time. By 431 BCE, the two city-states were once again at war with one another, but this time the conflict, which we now understand as the Peloponnesian War, would be much bloodier and longer, and it would help shape Greek history as well as the history of the entire ancient world.

The Spartans and the Peloponnesian League

The other main aggressor in the Peloponnesian War was the Spartans and their collection of allies known as the Peloponnesian League. However, unlike the Athenian-led Delian League, which emerged onto the scene in the 5th century BCE due to the looming threat of Persian invasion and that was designed as a way for member city-states to defend themselves, the Peloponnesian League dates back to the 6th century BCE and was designed to help Sparta retain control over the Peloponnese.

At the time, the Peloponnesian League would have been the oldest political organization in the Greek world. It was formed in 550 BCE to help the Spartans protect themselves against a potential revolt from Sparta's *helots*, the term used for agricultural laborers who were somewhere between serfs and slaves, and also to help defend against Argos, a city in the north of the Peloponnese that would have been Sparta's biggest rival at the time.

But in general, the Peloponnesian League was radically different from the Delian League. Whereas the Delian League was set up as a military alliance that had at its core the search for vengeance against the Persians, the Peloponnesian League was much more focused on the mutual defense of its members.

For example, the Delian League required payment of taxes or contributions of troops in order to be a member. But the Peloponnesian League made no such demand. Instead, member city-states were expected to give over troops whenever it was needed, and they could choose not to contribute to a campaign if they had good reason, which would have been almost exclusively religions, i.e., the gods did not permit war.

Another major difference between the Delian League and the Peloponnesian League was that there was no formal agreement between the city-states. Sparta was recognized as the League's hegemon, and each member's duties to the League were determined by negotiations made directly with Sparta. It's true that Athens eventually assumed a similar position in the Delian League, but the Delian League included city-states that would have rivaled Athens in power, which would have required a more collaborative approach. Sparta, on the other hand, was the agreed-upon hegemon and leader of the Peloponnesian League.

Yet despite lacking a formal agreement, there were several customs that each city-state would have been expected to uphold. For example, as mentioned earlier, each city-state would have been required to contribute troops when called upon. And each city-state participating in the Peloponnesian League was expected to take on the same friends and enemies as other members of the League. They would have also been asked to promise reciprocal assistance, meaning if someone helped you, you would have been responsible for helping them, and each city-state would have been asked to follow the military ambitions of the League's leader, i.e., Sparta. One interesting thing to note, though, is that there was nothing saying the members of the Peloponnesian League could not war with each other. And only Sparta was protected from having to act against its own interests.

Shortly after its formation, the League began to spread. Its first official member was Tegea which was forced to join after being defeated in battle against the Spartans. And by 510 BCE, the League covered the entire Peloponnese, and it even began to spread into other parts of Greece, specifically Attica, which is where Athens is located, as well as Boeotia where Thebes is.

Generally speaking, though, despite the dominance of Sparta, the League operated democratically. Each member city-state was given a vote, but Sparta did not participate in League voting. It determined its own course of action in the Spartan assembly, and the League meetings were more a chance for member states to decide how to best support Sparta in their military campaigns.

Overall, the organization of the Peloponnesian League helped turn this network of alliances into a powerful asset for Sparta during the Peloponnesian War. The League was always controlled by a Spartan, and as the conflict with Athens and the Delian League intensified, Sparta began installing military governors in League member states which made it easier for them to interfere in the domestic affairs of the city-states in the League. And it was this expansion of Spartan power that led to its attempt to secure greater control over Greece after their victory of the Athenians. However, similar to the Delian League, this ambition would prove to be their downfall, as several defeats left them quite weak to the advances of Philip of Macedon, the father of Alexander the Great, who would be the first person able to bring all of the mainland Greeks together under one empire.

Conclusion

The formation and the growth of the Delian and Peloponnesian Leagues is an important factor in the eventual break out of the Peloponnesian War. The Delian League came about as a result of a Greek alliance designed to help stop the Persian invasion, and the Spartan departure from this alliance helped set the stage for the Athenian rise to power.

Furthermore, each League helped provide wealth, troops, and strategic strongholds to both Sparta and Athens which they would use as a source of power and also as a means for waging war against one another for the better part of half a century.

However, the Delian League and the Peloponnesian League can also be seen as the downfall of both of these powerful Greek city-states. Because of their powerful position within the Delian League, Athenian strength would have been inflated in the minds of those in power. This, plus the need to seek revenge on the Persians, blinded the Athenians and caused them to embark on military campaigns against more powerful allies they likely never had much chance of winning.

And for the Spartans, the Peloponnesian League had never been much more than a loose, albeit effective, military coalition. However, after succeeding in securing their own power and then defeating the Athenians, this empowered them to continue their expansion, something that stretched them too thin and left them vulnerable to attack from the Macedonians, who were gaining in power whilst the Greeks fought amongst themselves. But no matter what, these two Leagues helped shape the history of the ancient world, and it was each one's quest for power and security that helped bring about the Peloponnesian War and shape the course of history.

Chapter 3 – Rising Tensions Between Athens and Sparta: The First Peloponnesian War to the Thirty Years' Peace

The Peloponnesian War is an important war in human history for a variety of reasons. Not only was it fought between two of the more powerful city-states in the Greek world at the time, thus redirecting the course of Greek history forever, but it was also one of the more well-documented wars of the ancient world.

Our modern-day concept of history is much different than that of the people living more than 2,000 years ago. To these early civilizations, history was far less grounded in fact. Traditions were passed down from generation to generation, a process known as oral history. However, over time, as people began to learn how to write and their grasp of language expanded, these histories were written down, and this gave those responsible for writing tremendous power over the nature of reality, for in the end, it was their interpretation of these oral histories that ended up defining the shape of that written history.

One of the world's first historians was Homer, and one of his most famous works, the *Iliad*, recounts some of the events surrounding one of the more famous conflicts of the ancient world, the Trojan War. However, most students of history do not consider this recounting to be history at all, but rather a story or a poem. A work of fiction. This is because the Trojan War likely never existed, at least not in the way Homer described it, and much of his interpretation is based on mythology and other nonrational beliefs.

But this should not discredit the significance of Homer's *Iliad*, for it instilled in Greek culture the need to write down and record the great events of the time. Much of what is known about the Greco-Persian Wars is because of the work of Herodotus, who many consider to be the first real historian. And our understanding of the Peloponnesian War comes largely from the work of Thucydides.

Other than the exceptional detail provided by Thucydides, who not only wrote about the events of the Peloponnesian War but who also even traveled to the locations of battles and to besieged cities to gather testimony and details about the events that transpired, Thucydides also spent a good deal of time analyzing and interpreting the events that led up to the war. And he did so in a way that is surprisingly reminiscent of how modern historians study war. He looked at the short-term, long-term, and necessary causes of war, the latter meaning those events that set a war in motion and made it impossible to stop. As a result, perhaps more so than with any other war in the ancient world, historians have been able to study the many different reasons as to why the Peloponnesian War broke out which helps us get a better understanding of the world at this time and also about why the war played out in the manner that it did.

Long-Term Causes of War

The long-term causes of war are those that have been developing, or brewing, for some time. And they are also those that allow people armed with hindsight to look back and declare war as "inevitable." Thucydides used this term to describe the Peloponnesian War, but it's likely he was using it more as a way of describing public opinion at the time in both Athens and Sparta, which, for a variety of reasons, would have wanted an "all or nothing" war with the other major Greek city-state.

In general, the largest long-term cause was most likely the rise of Athenian power. After having been successful in fighting back the Persian invasion and after becoming the focal point of the Delian League, Athens was morphing more into an empire than it had ever been before, and this likely would have terrified the Spartans. The reason this would have been so scary is that this would have put the Spartans directly in the sights of the Athenians.

Part of the reason for this was that the Spartans and Athenians had very different ambitions. The Spartans were far more interested in maintaining control over the Peloponnese and in maintaining control over the *helots*, the semi-free agricultural laborers who were responsible for working much of the land in the Peloponnese.

The Athenians, on the other hand, were becoming more concerned with expansion and imperialism. Their success in the Persian Wars had helped them make considerable gains in terms of their power, and they were witnessing firsthand how this power could be used to make the state more powerful, something that has caused many historians to call Athens one of the world's first "modern" states.

It should be clear, though, that these two strategies were in direct contrast with each other. The Spartans were most considered with consolidation and security, whereas the Athenians were much more concerned with expansion and imperialism. And given their close proximity, it can be safely concluded that these different ambitions put the two great city-states on a path for war which would eventually break out in 431 BCE.

However, there were other long-term causes to war other than diverging Spartan and Athenian interests. And it could be argued that these additional causes were even more powerful as they were mostly cultural.

Specifically, Thucydides cites a general appetite for war amongst the young males of both Spartans and Athens. Neither group would have had the chance to see significant conflict during their lives; the real fighting of the Greco-Persian Wars was some fifty years in the past, and the Thirty Years' Peace signed between Athens and Sparta in 446 BCE meant that there had been little in terms of conflict for most of the time that the young Greeks had been alive.

And this lack of conflict stirred up an emotional response in the Greek population that made war an attractive option, especially when taking into account how war was portrayed in Greek history or, more specifically, how it was glorified.

The publication of Homer's *Iliad* and its continued prominence in Greek culture helped establish a culture around war that promoted it as a way to achieve glory and excellence and also to prove one's manhood. And this idea was intensified after the Greco-Persian Wars. An image of brave Greeks coming together to defend their homeland in the face of a much larger and much more powerful Persian army helped to inspire young Greeks to seek an opportunity to prove their worth on the battlefield and to inscribe their names and identities into the annals of history.

But there is another factor at play that ties into this glorification of war, and it's one that had not really been seen in ancient cultures up until this point in time: freedom. The Greco-Persian Wars had been enshrined in the collective Greek consciousness as a defense of freedom against the tyranny of foreign invaders. But this understanding of freedom was colored depending on the city-state to which each Greek citizen pledged allegiance.

For example, as mentioned earlier, Athenians had begun to see some of the benefits that could come from amassing power and stretching imperial influence, and this caused them to associate the ideas of freedom into the expansion of Athenian influence, the idea being that it was far easier to be free as a ruler than as the ruled. And this notion of freedom as being something earned by the rulers was combined with the growing presence of democratic ideals and institutions in Athenian society, providing a strong justification for continued warfare against neighboring civilizations that were a threat to Athenian autonomy.

However, in Sparta, this idea of freedom would have been understood much more differently. As a society much more concerned with maintaining the status quo and protecting their stronghold in the Peloponnese, freedom would have been understood as something that needed to be defended, not won. They too saw freedom more accessible as the ruler instead of the ruled, but they felt no need to extend their own power to protect this status as the ruler. But with the Athenians growing ever more ambitious, it would have certainly felt like this autonomy was in jeopardy, setting the stage for war.

A good example of how this dichotomy played out can be seen with how the Athenians dealt with some of the rebellions that took place within the Delian League after its formation and before the outbreak of war. Two city-states, Thasos and Samos, rebelled from the Athenian-ruled Delian League in 466/465 BCE and 440/439 BCE, respectively. And the Athenian response to these insurrections was harsh. Treasuries were emptied, and armed forces were required to retire. The Athenians, who saw their power as their only avenue to freedom, would have wanted to crush these rebellions so as to maintain their grip on power. However, this action sent a message to other city-states around Greece: the Athenians were looking for conquest, and they weren't afraid of the consequences.

This would have struck fear in other city-states interested in exerting some of their own autonomy but who found themselves allied or bound to Athens either formally, as a member of the Delian League, or informally as a tributary. And this fear would have encouraged those under Athenian influence to begin to look elsewhere for assistance which in time would come from the Spartans and the Peloponnesian League.

Looking back at how the Peloponnesian War developed, it's easy to see how it had been brewing for decades before the fighting broke out. But this general trend toward war should not be interpreted as an inevitability. It took the right combination of ambition and directed action to turn this collective appetite for war into a conscious decision to take up arms and fight.

The First Peloponnesian War

It may seem a bit confusing to refer to the main conflict between the Athenians and the Spartans as the Peloponnesian War and then to name the conflict that took place some fifteen years earlier the "First Peloponnesian War," but this is how historians have always done it. This could be because Thucydides was the first person to refer to these series of conflicts as the "Peloponnesian War." However, he excluded the conflicts that took place in the "First Peloponnesian War." This may have been because these initial conflicts rarely took place directly between Spartans and Athenians but rather their allies. As a result, these conflicts were excluded from Thucydides' account of the "Peloponnesian War," but historians consider this initial confrontation to be important, and since it was fought between the same adversaries, it has been dubbed the "First Peloponnesian War."

However, no matter how confusing the names are, this initial set of conflicts is crucial to the Peloponnesian War. It marked the beginning of hostilities between the two powerful city-states, and it helped to outline some of the alliances that would eventually help to define the war. As a result, it's important to study at least the overarching themes of this war as well as some of its key events so as to better understand the Peloponnesian War and why it broke out when it did.

But, to skip to the end, part of the reason the First Peloponnesian War is so important is that it led to the "Thirty Years' Peace" treaty. This is significant because in the years leading up to the Peloponnesian War both sides would claim that the other had broken the terms of this treaty and that they were not acting in good faith, which both sides used as a justification for taking up arms against the other. However, when we look at how the First Peloponnesian War unfolded and how it came to an end, it's easy to see why this peace treaty did not last and why it was broken in favor of a much larger and much bloodier conflict that would reshape the events of Greek history moving forward.

The First Peloponnesian War came about for reasons not so dissimilar to those of the Peloponnesian War. Essentially, Sparta's growing envy of the Athenian Empire, which was expanding in terms of both territory and cultural influence, pushed it into conflict with the Athenians so as to protect its own freedom and autonomy. But rather interestingly, the beginning of this war saw these future rivals actually fighting on the same side. Specifically, the Spartans were facing a large-scale revolt from the *helots*, and in an effort to stop this rebellion, they called upon their old allies from the times of fighting the Persians which included the Athenians.

Surprisingly, the Athenians agreed and sent an army to the Peloponnese to help the Spartans deal with their internal strife, but these soldiers were sent home nearly as soon as they arrived, and they were the only ones to be sent home which sent the signal to Athens that the Athenians were not welcome in Sparta. This move was not received well in Athens, and perhaps fearing that Sparta's action was a masked declaration of war, the Athenian response was to seek alliances with some of Sparta's rivals in the region.

Specifically, Athens made alliances with Thessaly, a powerful city-state in northern Greece, Argos, an enemy of Sparta for centuries, and Megara, a former ally of Sparta's that had been fighting and losing a border war with Corinth, the most powerful city in between Athens and Sparta that had declared its allegiance to Sparta. Athens also began settling the helots who had revolted but been defeated, giving them a place to live and work and further exacerbating Spartan resentment of the Athenians.

By 460 BCE, the Spartans and the Athenians were at war, although they rarely engaged one another directly. Instead, most of the fighting took place in what was essentially a proxy war. In other words, Athens would support enemies of Sparta and vice versa. However, the two did engage in the Battle of Tanagra which Sparta won, despite the fact that Athens had formed an alliance with Argos, the second most powerful city-state in the Peloponnesian League and the only real threat to Spartan power in the League. An Athenian victory in Oenophyta helped the Athenians conquer nearly all of Boeotia except for Thebes. And the Athenians followed this success by sending ships to circumnavigate the Peloponnese and ravage the Spartan ports and docks. This led to the conquest of Chalcis on the Corinthian Gulf which would have put the Spartans in a remarkably difficult position.

However, as is often the case in wars of conquest, the Athenians had overextended themselves. Staying true to the original purpose of the Delian League, which was formed in part to exact revenge on the Persians for their invasion of Greece, the Athenians had supported a rebellion in Egypt. Initial success came to a screeching halt in 454 BCE when the Persian general, Megabyzus, routed the combined Egyptian and Athenian forces. This devastated the Athenian fleet and put their control over the Aegean, which was the main source of their power, wealth, and influence in the region, at risk. They therefore withdrew their forces from Egypt and began focusing on maintaining their power.

The first step in doing this was to negotiate peace with the Persians, thus bringing an end to the Greco-Persian Wars. This occurred in 449 BCE, and the next few years brought on even more instability within Greece. Sparta, in an attempt to undermine Athenian power, declared Delphi, the city where the Oracle of Delphi resided, independent from Phocis, a move that displeased the Athenians who considered Delphian independence to be of the utmost importance.

This was followed by a revolt in 447 BCE throughout Boeotia. The Athenians attempted to stop this revolt by sending out an army, but they were defeated which effectively ended the Athenian Empire in mainland Greece (the Athenian Empire existed mostly in the Aegean Islands and Ionia). But these rebellions inspired even more insurrection in territories recently conquered by Athens, such as Megara, and this left the Athenians in a very difficult situation. The Spartans invaded Attica, the region where Athens was located, but were pushed back.

However, by 446 BCE, it was evident that nothing was going to come from this near constant conflict between the Athenians and Spartans, and a truce was formalized into a treaty known as the "Thirty Years' Peace."

Breaking the Peace and the Start of the War

This treaty was signed in the winter of 446/445 BCE, and as the name suggests, it was meant to last thirty years. However, it would barely last half that time, with fighting breaking out once again in 431 BCE. However, in the beginning, the treaty served its purpose. It stopped the continuous hostilities that are referred to collectively as the First Peloponnesian War.

But knowing some of the long-term causes addressed above, it's clear that the First Peloponnesian War did not do enough to settle the boiling tensions that existed between the Spartans and the Athenians. The Athenians were still the most powerful member of the Delian League, and they were still using this power to assert their imperialistic ambitions throughout the Aegean. As a result, it should come as no surprise that this peace treaty would not last, although it certainly was effective in staving off war for at least some time.

The terms of the treaty are important to consider. First, Athens was forced to give up nearly all of its possessions in the Peloponnese, which makes sense considering the Spartans' primary objective all along had been to try and limit Athenian expansion into their territory. Furthermore, the treaty stipulated that war between the two city-states could not occur if one of the two sides asserted that it wanted to settle a debate with arbitration, which would require calling in a third party to help detail and enforce terms.

As war approached, Athens would claim that Sparta denied it the chance to settle conflicts in arbitration, but many historians believe this was nothing more than propaganda intended to drum up support for the war with Sparta and to position Sparta as the aggressors. And this claim makes sense when taking into account the actions of both Sparta and Athens in the years both directly after the signing of the Thirty Years' Peace and also those leading up to the outbreak of the Peloponnesian War.

The first breakdown in the truce created by the Thirty Years' Peace occurred in 440 BCE, just five years after the treaty was made official. Samos, a strong ally of Athens, revolted against Athenian rule after having been made promises by the Persian satrap in Asia Minor. Word of the revolt spread, and it looked as though Athens' grip on power was in serious jeopardy. Many historians believe that had Sparta intervened on the side of those revolting against the Athenians then they may have been able to deal a crushing blow to Athens that would have made the Peloponnesian War unnecessary.

Recognizing this opportunity, the Spartans called a congress made up of all the members of the Peloponnesian League to discuss the possibility of resuming conflict with Athens, but this motion was voted down with the assembly choosing instead to honor the terms of the Thirty Years' Peace. The Corinthians, who were always in the middle of Athenian and Spartan conflicts, were opposed to war, and many scholars believe this is the main reason why Sparta chose not to go to war with Athens again at this time.

The very fact that Sparta was considering war with Athens just five years after enacting the Thirty Years' Peace should shed some light on just how precarious this peace was and also on how doomed the treaty was. And the next major conflict to erupt in Greece would put this peace to the test once again, yet this time things would not turn out so well, and the result would be the outbreak of the Peloponnesian War.

The next conflict that tested the peace and that eventually led to resumed fighting between the Athenians and Spartans was the war that broke out between Corcyra and Corinth over the colony Epidamnos, a far and distant land in present-day Albania. The Corcyreans had established a colony there for trade, and it was ruled by a closed, tight-knit oligarchy. However, as the colony became wealthier over time, merchants inside the city began to push for more democratic rule, and they appealed to Corinth for support in their effort.

This move put Corinth and Corcyra in direct opposition to one another, and knowing the Corinthians to be longtime allies of the Spartans and members of the Peloponnesian League, the Corcyreans appealed to the Athenians for help. Their argument to sway the Athenians into the conflict was that there were three great naval fleets in Greece at the time. The Athenians had one, and so did the Corinthians, but the Corinthians were already aligned with the Spartans. However, the third great fleet was that of Corcyra, and the Corcyreans made the case that they alone could not beat the Corinthians, meaning that if the Athenians did not come to their aid then the Corinthian and the Corcyrean fleet would end up merging into one, putting the Athenians at a severe disadvantage in any future wars against the Peloponnesians.

The Athenians saw the logic in this argument and pledged their support to Corcyra, but they attempted to appease both sides by agreeing only to provide defensive units, pledging that they would not go on the offensive. However, when Athenian forces arrived in Epidamnos, they were unable to resist the call to war, and they ended up attacking, and the Battle of Sybota in 433 BCE took place between Corinthian and Athenian forces, putting more strain on the Thirty Years' Peace than ever before.

This conflict was exacerbated even more when Athens decided to punish those who had come to the defense of Corinth during this battle, most notably Megara. The Athenians enacted trade sanctions against Megara, which was an ally of both Corinth and Sparta. Furthermore, the Athenians attacked the colony of Potidaea in 432 BCE after it decided to rebel against Athens and the Delian League in an attempt to secede from the alliance. This move was supported by Corinth, which once again put Athens in direct conflict with close allies of Sparta.

Seeing that the Athenians had no real intention of maintaining the Thirty Years' Peace, the Spartans sent several envoys to Athens throughout 432 and 431 BCE hoping to engage the Athenians in diplomatic conversations. However, the Athenians refused the envoys, saying that the Spartans were not willing to engage in arbitration which the Athenians were demanding and which they had the right to demand according to the Thirty Years' Peace. Most of these envoys asked the Athenians to abandon some of their support for conflicts involving Spartan allies, but these were either ignored or refused.

Also, in 432 BCE, the Spartans called together a congress of the Peloponnesian League after the Corinthians had requested them to do so. This was meant to be an opportunity for different members of the League to voice their grievances against the Athenians which was designed to encourage the Spartans to end their inactivity and take arms up against the Athenians.

For obvious reasons, the Athenians were not invited, yet they showed up anyway, and this gave way to a famous debate between the Athenians and Corinthians which Thucydides recorded. In this debate, the Corinthians called out the Spartans for not taking enough action, and that if they wanted to continue to stand on the sidelines while Athens made moves throughout Greece, then they would soon find themselves without allies and in a difficult position to defend their own homeland. The Athenians, on the other hand, warned the entire Peloponnesian League of the dangers involved in going to war with such a powerful state, harking back to their victories over the Persians so as to strike fear in the different member city-states and discourage them from war, suggesting that the Spartans instead engage in arbitration. However, this threat proved to not have the intended effect, and the majority of the Peloponnesian League voted that Athens had broken the peace. The Athenians then used this refusal to arbitrate as a way of positioning the Spartans as the aggressors.

However, most historians agree that this claim about arbitration was nothing more than a ploy to convince the people that war was necessary. Athens had risen to power throughout the 5th century BCE and was seeing that power crumble. It made no sense, within the Athenian framework, to sue for peace, as doing so would mean once again accepting the limits to their power. But for Sparta, peace made sense, since they were more interested in maintaining their autonomy and had little desire to expand their sphere of influence.

Because of this, the argument could most certainly be made that war was indeed inevitable. The Spartans were attempting to negotiate peace, and the Athenians were simultaneously allegedly asking for arbitration. Yet neither was willing to listen to the other, and Sparta's powerful allies had no real interest in peace after all that Athens had done to them during the time of the Thirty Years' Peace.

Some historians have argued that attempts were made at arbitration but that there was no third party deemed suitable to serve as the arbiter. But even had they found a way to negotiate peace once again, the network of alliances and the many different competing interests of both Athens and Sparta put these two city-states, and those they were connected to, at odds with one another, and looking back, it's easy to see how war was the only way to solve this conflict.

Necessary Causes of War

In 431 BCE, tensions were hot. Despite the Thirty Years' Peace, Athens and Sparta were essentially at war once again. The Spartan vote declaring that the Athenians had broken the peace all but declared war, but the two sides had not yet engaged in direct conflict. Athens was fighting the Corinthians, a powerful ally of the Spartans, but no battle had taken place between Spartan and Athenian forces. For this to happen, it would take something to push these tensions over the top, meaning someone would need to break the stalemate.

Somewhat interestingly, the event that would end the dance between Sparta and Athens and send them to war was not all that different from the event that turned the arms races of the 19th century into an all-out total war. But instead of an assassination, the event was a "sneak attack."

Sometime in 431 BCE, a force of around 300 Thebans from the city-state of Thebes, a powerful ally of Sparta and the Peloponnesian League, entered the city of Plataea. They were given access to the city by private citizens who were expecting this force to kill the leadership in Plataea so that Plataea, which at the time was allied with Athens, and Thebes could enter an alliance. But the citizenry turned against this Theban force and killed them all in the night.

The Athenians sent several envoys to Plataea to try and mitigate the effects of this move, but these had little or no effect. Thebes continued to send military support to Plataea, but these were nearly all fought back, and Thebes suffered heavy losses. After some time, the Spartans sent reinforcements, and so did the Athenians, and war was on.

It's difficult to say why this attack was more serious and more impactful than others, but it's likely that this was simply the straw that broke the camel's back. Thebes had always been one of the more powerful cities in Ancient Greece, and it's likely this betrayal and subsequent series of defeats was simply too much for the Thebans, the Spartans, and the rest of the Peloponnesian League. But no matter the exact reason, this event set in motion the Peloponnesian War which would last for the next 27 years and would completely reshape the history of ancient Greece and the world.

Conclusion

Looking back with the lens of history, it's quite easy to see how this war was inevitable. Differing interests combined with tenuous alliances made for a precarious geopolitical situation in Greece during the 5ᵗʰ century BCE. Both Sparta and Athens were simply too powerful to coexist, but because of the difficult nature of Greek geography and political organization, it was impossible for either one of them to be able to amass enough power and influence to completely overcome the other one.

As a result, these two powers, despite being allies during the Persian invasions of Greece, became bitter enemies. The vast majority of the Greek world would be sucked into this conflict with nearly every city-state being required to pick a side, a decision that would end up having a significant impact on not only their own future but that of the entire Greek civilization. However, for as interesting as this conflict has been up until now, it is really just beginning.

Chapter 4 – The Archidamian War to the Peace of Nicias

In total, the Peloponnesian War lasted 27 years, and part of the reason we even use this name is because that is what Thucydides called it when he was putting together his now-famous historical account of the conflict. However, these 27 years were not filled with continuous conflict. Fighting broke out in 431 BCE with the Theban attack on Plataea, and this would continue for the next ten years until the Peace of Nicias brought the conflict to a temporary end. This period of the Peloponnesian War is usually referred to as the Ten Years' War, or also the Archidamian War, named after Sparta's king at the time, Archidamus II.

In these ten years of the war, Sparta was mostly on the offensive, while Athens was largely on the defensive, although a brief change in this dynamic would have a dramatic impact on how this part of the war would play out. Specifically, an Athenian victory near Sparta proper incited new support for the war and pushed it to different theaters, a move that would end up defining these initial ten years of war.

Throughout the conflict, it would become apparent just how difficult it would be for either side to gain a significant advantage. Sparta relied on its superior land force, while Athens relied on its naval fleets. Yet this difference would end up being an important part of the overall Peloponnesian War, as it exacerbated the tensions between the two sides and set them up for nearly two more decades of conflict. And this continuous conflict would help to reshape not only Greek warfare but also its art and philosophy, both of which would go on to have major influences in shaping the world in which we live today.

The War Begins

Although the "sneak attack" that took place in Plataea in 431 BCE officially set the Peloponnesian War in motion, it would still be some time before the two sides involved—Athens and Sparta— would engage in a decisive battle, and this was largely due to the dramatically different strengths of each city-state.

More specifically, Athens was a naval power, whereas Sparta derived its dominance from its massive, well-trained armies; the Spartan military has been regarded by historians as one of the finest of the ancient world. And while each of these strengths would allow both sides to inflict serious damage on the other, a decisive battle would not take place for many years. And it only happened years into the war largely because of a change in strategy that resulted from a transition in Athenian leadership which will be discussed shortly.

But before this would happen, the battle that was taking place at Plataea needed to be finished. After the attack by the Plataeans against the Theban envoy, both Sparta and Athens sent forces to help ease tensions. Most of the Thebans were trapped and detained, but several were able to escape, and they returned with a large force that immediately put the city under siege. The small Athenian force that was there fought valiantly to defend the city, but by the middle of 427 BCE, the Spartans broke through the walls and pillaged the city, killing survivors and razing buildings. Because of this, Plataea was all but destroyed, but the Athenians had sent too few forces in support of Plataea for this defeat to have a large effect on their overall victory.

However, while Athens was attempting to try and defend Plataea, two other things were happening in the war that were helping to shape its early history. First, the Athenians, under the leadership of Pericles, had decided to adopt a defensive strategy in which Athens would protect itself and its most important allies using its naval power while also attacking strategic ports along the coast of the Peloponnese to try and weaken Spartan power. This strategy discouraged Athenians from engaging with Spartans in open battle, and this caused most Athenians living in the fields outside the city to abandon their homes and seek refuge inside the city walls of Athens, which had been built long and tall so as to protect the city and also its port, Piraeus.

This left much of the land on Attica completely open, which the Spartans promptly invaded and burned. They cut down grape trees, destroyed farms, burned forests, and knocked down houses, but they killed very few people. And because Athens still had access to the sea, its position was not weakened by these Spartan advances. Also, because early Spartan warfare traditions had Spartan armies return for the harvest season because helot revolts in the Peloponnese were a constant concern for the Spartans, they were never able to occupy Attica and Athenian lands for more than forty days at a time, which would have significantly reduced the risk they faced of invasion.

However, the second thing that happened both during and after the long siege of Plataea actually had nothing to do with war. A plague broke out in Athens in 430 BCE that would prove to be devastating. Athens was already crowded, but once war with the Spartans began, those living in the fields surrounding the city began making their way inside the city walls, which made it easy for disease to spread even more quickly, especially since sanitation and medicine at this time were still relatively primitive.

It's estimated that the plague killed between one-third and two-thirds of the Athenian population between 430 and 427 BCE. This is significant not only because it would have greatly reduced the number of people upon which the Athenian leadership could call upon to fight, but it also discouraged many Athenian allies from offering their support. Plague in ancient times was no joke, and no one would have wanted to get too close to a city being ravished by it, for this could easily cause the plague and all its devastation to spread to another city.

Furthermore, in addition to losing a huge chunk of its population, Athens also lost its leader at the time, Pericles, to the plague. Pericles was not only well-respected and revered within Athens, but he was also a skilled military commander who knew how to play to his own strengths while not exposing himself too much to those of the enemy. In short, the defensive strategy that Athens took on in the beginning part of the war, which, had it not been for the plague, was rather successful, was really the idea of Pericles. And when he died, so did the approach taken by Athenian leadership, which would dramatically alter the course of the war.

Athenian Aggression

After Pericles died, a man named Cleon took over. He was a member of the more hawkish factions within the Athenian government, and so once he was named leader, he immediately began implementing a more aggressive strategy against the Spartans. And while this might have produced initial successes, it can just as easily be seen as a turning point that set Athens on a path for defeat in this first part of the conflict and perhaps also the entire Peloponnesian War.

But before going too far into what Cleon and his military general, Demosthenes, did to Sparta, it's important to look at the Spartan system, as this helps shed some light on where their weakness were and why the Athenians chose the approach they did.

As mentioned earlier, the strength of Sparta was their military. Boys were chosen early on to be soldiers, and they would be sent away to properly train, turning the Spartan army into a true professional army. It's true these soldiers still had duties at home, e.g., they were supposed to return each year to assist with the harvest, but generally speaking, they would leave their homes for most of the year so that they could be involved in the various campaigns being conducted around the Peloponnese and the rest of Greece.

This system, while effective at helping the Spartans build a strong military, left them vulnerable as they needed to rely on slave labor to help them tend to their fields and grow their food. These slaves, known as helots, were a constant challenge in maintaining peace in the Peloponnese since they would rebel almost any time they had the chance to do so, which left Sparta constantly exposed to not only internal strife but also manpower shortages—if the helots revolted, supplies became scarce in and around Sparta, and the military would also get distracted by the need to quell the rebellion.

But before the Athenians could take advantage of these weaknesses, they would need to spend some time pushing the Spartans back in other areas of Greece. For example, they began running some campaigns in both Boeotia (the region where Thebes is located), as well as Aetolia (see map below for details), which helped to push the Spartans back. However, it was the events that would take place in Aegean, specifically on the island of Lesbos, one of the largest and most important Athenian strongholds in the Aegean Sea, that would best demonstrate Athenian aggression at this point of the war.

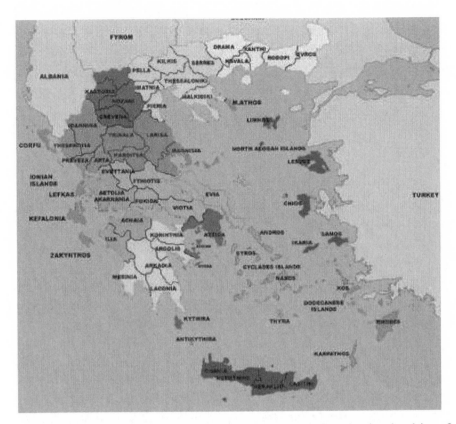

One of the city-states on Lesbos, Mytilene, under the leadership of the oligarchs living there who were hoping to take control over the democratic Athenians, rebelled in 428 BCE. And since they knew Athens and Sparta were at war, these oligarchs appealed to the Spartans for help, which they got. However, it was not enough, and the Athenian response was ruthless but not as ruthless as it could have been. Cleon wanted to kill all the adult men and enslave the rest of the population, but the Athenian assembly, which was growing tired of Cleon's aggression, voted to kill *just* the 1,000 people who were considered responsible for the revolt.

This rebuttal of Cleon's wishes represents a big part of the problem with the Athenian strategy at the time. The war with Sparta was proving to be rather futile. Neither was making any real progress, and the hardship experienced by both sides' general population was beginning to become unbearable. As a result, there was an appetite for peace, especially in Athens, but Cleon, who still had considerable influence, wanted no part in this, so he continued advancing on the Spartans, hoping a military success would reinvigorate the people and help him win their support for continuing the war.

Pylos and Sphacteria

As mentioned earlier, part of the Athenian strategy was to use their naval fleet to attack the various Spartan outposts on the coast of the Peloponnese. And as the Athenians approached the post of Pylos, which was near the tiny island of Sphacteria, they began to feel hope toward their efforts against the Spartans, largely because as the Athenians won small battles on the coast, helots, desperate to be free from their masters and willing to support anyone who might provide it, flocked toward the Athenian strongholds. This left Sparta in a difficult situation, as this meant there was no one left to tend to the fields and supply the armies.

Because of the Athenian presence in Pylos, it quickly became a hotspot for helot runaways. Interestingly, the Athenians ended up in Pylos by accident. Their fleet had been blown ashore by a storm, and the Athenian commander, Demosthenes, ordered the troops to fortify the peninsula, which established one of the few Athenian outposts in Spartan territory at this point in the war.

When this happened, helots from all over the Peloponnese made a run toward Pylos thinking that doing so would bring them freedom. This threatened the Spartan system of slave labor, which was its greatest weakness as they heavily depended on it. Because of this, Sparta would need to respond if it hoped to keep the helots under control and maintain its own grip on power. And the Spartan decision led to the Battle of Pylos, one of the few direct engagements between the Athenians and Spartans in the early years of the war.

The battle, which took place in 425 BCE, was fought almost entirely at sea, which gave the Athenians, with their much larger, much stronger fleet, a significant advantage that they used to win a decisive victory at Pylos. In fact, their victory was so swift that the Spartans were left in a difficult position. They had put a force of 420 hoplites (the term used for well-trained, professional Greek soldiers) on the island of Sphacteria, which was just outside the harbor of Pylos, and when the Athenians swooped in with their large fleet, these soldiers were trapped.

This terrified Spartan leaders largely because 120 of these soldiers were of the Spartiate class, which was the highest in both the Spartan army and society. These soldiers had been handpicked at a young age to be great warriors, and significant amounts of time and resources were dedicated to turning them into elite warriors. Losing over 100 of these world-class soldiers would have been a devastating setback. So, to prevent this from happening, Spartan leaders arrived at Pylos to negotiate an armistice that would lead to the safe return of these soldiers.

To help show that the Spartans were negotiating in good faith, they surrendered their entire fleet at Pylos to the Athenians. Then, the Spartan leaders were sent back to Athens to work toward a lasting peace deal, but these negotiations failed. And when this happened, the Athenians retained the surrendered fleet and launched a siege on Sphacteria, which eventually became known as the Battle of Sphacteria.

Unsurprisingly, given that the Spartans had surrendered their fleet and also that the Athenians had a huge naval advantage, the hoplites on Sphacteria surrendered. They were taken as prisoners of war and returned to Athens.

Overall, this had two huge effects. First, it gave the Athenians a stronghold in the Peloponnese that was rather close to Sparta itself. This not only made it easier for them to run raids all around the Peloponnese as a way of weakening Spartan power, but it also gave rebelling helots a place to run to and find refuge from their Spartan masters, which would put the stability of Spartan society at great risk.

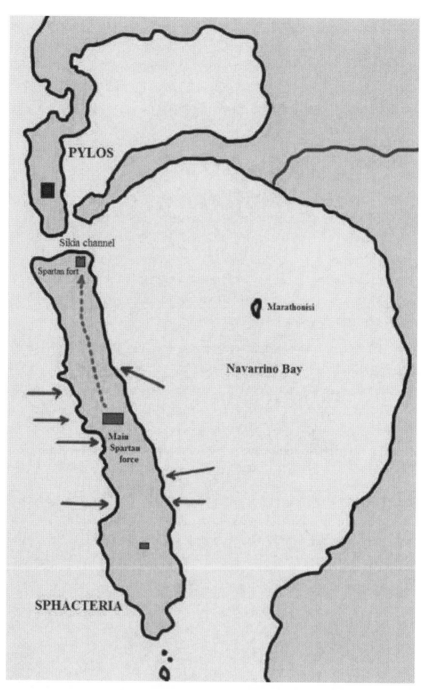

But the second main effect of the Athenian successes at Pylos and Sphacteria was that it gave the Athenians great hope that victory over the Spartans could actually happen. They had never before been able to defeat a Spartan army and take its hoplites as prisoners, and doing so gave credence to Cleon's aggressive strategy, which he would continue implementing after these victories until eventually he would stretch himself too far and put all of Athens in grave danger. Below are maps of Greece as well as the island of Sphacteria, which help show both why the Athenians were able to win and also why the Spartans were so concerned with this particular defeat.

Amphipolis and Brasidas

Threatened by the Athenian success in the Peloponnese, the Spartans needed to find a way to retaliate. And since their naval forces were considerably weaker than the Athenians, they knew this needed to happen somewhere where the Athenians would be forced to fight on land.

After some debate, the Spartan general Brasidas convinced the ruling parties in Sparta to authorize an expedition to northern Greece. He claimed he would be able to achieve a victory similar to those won by Cleon in the Peloponnese and that this would help stave off Athenian advances by forcing them to pay attention to other theaters of the war.

In general, Brasidas is considered one of the more skilled military commanders Sparta has ever produced, and this helped him deliver on the promises he made. He and his army marched all the way to Amphipolis, which was a strategic city in the northern Aegean, and they were able to quickly and easily capture it. Interestingly enough, the Athenian general who was responsible for defending the city was Thucydides, but he was unable to arrive at the city fast enough to stop the Spartans, and this defeat forced him to give up his duties as a military commander. And when this happened, he turned to writing history, with his first work being *The Peloponnesian War*, which is the main source used for any study about this tremendous conflict of the ancient world.

But for as good as Brasidas was at commanding an army, he was also a skilled diplomat. After winning Amphipolis, Brasidas used his moderate approach to win over the support of the people, both in Amphipolis as well as many of the other city-states in the region. This threatened Athenian control in the region, which would have threatened the entirety of their power since it depended almost exclusively on the islands of the Aegean for its wealth and resources.

However, part of the reason Brasidas was able to do this is that the people's appetite for war had waned considerably since fighting and disease had broken out in 431 and 430 BCE respectively. Anyone aware of what was going on could see that little was being gained by either side and that the very fabric of Greek society was being threatened. In fact, many historians believe that had the Athenians failed at Pylos they would have been forced to sue for peace by their own people. But because they didn't the conflict continued, and this led to the Spartan invasion of Amphipolis and the nearby city-states.

Another interesting point about this particular moment in the war is that Brasidas was leading an army consisting mainly of freed helots. This suggests that the Spartans were aware of the fragility of their social structure and also on how easily they could be deprived of the manpower needed to support their war effort. Spartan society had been built on the slave labor of helots, so this stark about-face in their helot policy should be taken as a recognition by Spartan leadership of their primary weakness. And this decision makes a lot of sense. Freeing helots not only expanded the pool upon which Spartan authorities could draw their armies, but this also helped to quell some of the discontent that existed in Spartan society that threatened to undermine their war efforts from within.

However, unlike Sparta, Athens was not as good at recognizing its own weaknesses, and this would help to change the direction of the war once again. The Athenians had been led by Cleon in their victories of Pylos and Sphacteria, and this must have given him the idea that he was a skilled military commander, which Thucydides mocks in his account, stating that Cleon's successes were more the result of the massive advantage the Athenians held than Cleon's prowess as a soldier and general.

Nevertheless, as the leader of the Athenian assembly, he could easily win support for his campaigns, and he decided that he would be the one to lead a counterattack in Amphipolis, which was designed to remove Brasidas from power and restore Athenian influence in the region. However, it would take him until 422 BCE to summon the army and the support needed for this campaign, and by the time he arrived in the northern Aegean, he had a much larger force than Brasidas, but his adversary was deeply entrenched, and they had considerable support from the people who were living there.

As a result, it should not be seen as a huge surprise that Cleon and his Athenian forces were beaten back and ended up being forced to flee. Yet Brasidas was wounded early in the battle, and he died by the time it ended. But perhaps more importantly, Cleon was killed as he and his troops were retreating, and this opened the door for a new leader in Athens, and this time moderation would win out, which would help bring this chapter of the war to a close.

The Peace of Nicias

As mentioned earlier, Cleon rose to power on the backs of a hawkish caucus that had been gaining in popularity and power within the Athenian assembly. His adversaries, who were more moderate and less apt to continue the war, were forced into silence while Cleon was in power. However, when he died, the appetite for war had waned, and the moderates were able to put one of their own, Nicias, at the head of the government. He himself was far more moderate, and he used his newfound power to sue for peace with Sparta.

In the end, this peace treaty, which was signed in 421 BCE, became known as the Peace of Nicias, largely because he was the one responsible for brokering it; however, this probably gives him too much credit. War weariness at this point in the conflict was extremely high, and Sparta had been suing for peace for some time, and they had been doing so aggressively since their soldiers had been captured on Sphacteria. It was really the ego and ambition of Cleon and those around him that continued the war, and so with him out of the way, one could almost say that an agreement was inevitable.

The terms of the treaty were meant to establish peace between the two powerful city-states for at least fifty years, and it was meant to restore things to how they were before the war had begun. But of course, there were to be a few exceptions. For example, Thebes retained Plataea, which is interesting since this attack was considered by many to be the impetus for war. Additionally, Athens kept control over some of the Corinthian territories it had won in Western

Greece, and the Spartans agreed to abandon some of the communities that they had taken over near Amphipolis as a result of Brasidas' military and diplomatic leadership.

However, in this process, Athens was forced to acknowledge some of the freedoms, largely in terms of land ownership and taxes, Brasidas had granted these communities, and that made it difficult for Athens to ever retain the same level of control over these territories as it had before the war broke out. Lastly, the peace treaty made it clear that Athens and Sparta would need to impose acceptance of these terms upon their allies, or their respective leagues, so that fighting would not break out once again as a result of conflicting alliances.

Conclusion

The Peace of Nicias brought the war to an end for the time being, but it was far from a permanent settlement. Looking back, its only real purpose is to provide a good place to break up the 27 years of conflict that would eventually become known as the Peloponnesian War, and it's why this part of the war is often referred to as the "Stalemate."

It's true that leaders at the time might have looked at this agreement as a step in the right direction, but most historians today consider this treaty to have actually exacerbated many of the tensions in the Greek peninsula, which effectively set the Hellenic people up for much more conflict down the road.

The main reason for this is the way in which the treaty essentially reorganized Greek society so that Athens and Sparta were the two superpowers. As mentioned earlier, Athens and Sparta had to impose acceptance of the treaty upon their allies, and this would have threatened the autonomy of those city-states who participated in their respective leagues not because they were coerced but rather because it was in their interest to do so. Specifically, Corinth and Megara were particularly displeased with the Peace of Nicias, and this tension would bubble for several years until fighting would once again break out and the great Peloponnesian War would continue.

However, perhaps the most important takeaway from this part of the war is the difference in each side's strengths. Athenian naval power discouraged them from ever attacking on land, and Sparta's strength on land would forever put them at a disadvantage in sea battles. This made it hard for either side to engage in a decisive battle, which is part of the reason this war dragged on for so long.

Furthermore, Athens' weak infantry meant that it could not properly defend the land surrounding its city, which exposed Athens proper to overpopulation and disease. But Sparta was not without its own internal strife. The helots were a constant problem for the Spartans, and it wasn't until a shift in their policy toward the helots as well as in their military strategy that they were able to make more significant progress in their fight against the Athenians. And as one might expect, these issues would not go away as the war continued and eventually built up toward an ending that would alter the course of the ancient world and the many civilizations that would come later.

Chapter 5 – The Attack of Syracuse Brings More War

By 421 BCE, the Peace of Nicias had helped bring a temporary stop to the fighting between Athens and Sparta, but as should be evident by now, it did not succeed in halting conflict amongst the Greek people. The power and authority afforded to both Athens and Sparta upset the other powers in the Greek world, and this would help to stir up more conflict after the peace.

However, perhaps more importantly, the Peace of Nicias, or the first ten years of the Peloponnesian War for that matter, did not produce a resolution for the main driver of conflict: the expansion of Athenian power at the expense of Spartan autonomy. Athens was intent on maintaining and expanding its empire, and the complicated network of alliances that existed among the countless Greek city-states meant that nearly every attempt to do this could somehow be interpreted as an attempt to limit Spartan independence and power.

As a result, it's tough to believe that anyone at the time really thought the war was over for good. This is because as long as Athens continued to try and expand its influence in the region, there would likely be conflict. And since Athens depended on this influence for both wealth and resources, they had no real incentive to stop, putting the Hellenic people on a crash course for more conflict and causing the Peloponnesian War to continue and begin moving toward its end.

However, unlike the first part of the Peloponnesian War, this next stage of the conflict does not have its own name, largely because there is no peace treaty or pause in fighting that helps break up the conflict. However, one name that is often used is the "Interlude." It starts with the Peace of Nicias and goes through the Athenian expedition to Syracuse. We can consider this the second phase of the war, with the following phase considered to be the decisive phase, sometimes earning the name "Drive to Decision." Breaking the war up into these different segments makes it not only easier to understand but also helps clarify why the conflict lasted so long and why it eventually ended the way it did. But before the war would resume, some geopolitical tensions throughout Greece would flare up and set the stage for part two of the Peloponnesian War.

Athens and Argos Make an Alliance

As mentioned earlier, Corinth was most displeased with the arrangement brokered between Athens and Sparta. Corinth had been a longtime ally of Sparta and a member of the Peloponnesian League, but as a powerful city-state in its own right, it also felt that it did not have to answer to Sparta. Yet the imposition of peace by Sparta as a result of the Peace of Nicias threatened this autonomy and put the Corinthians in a difficult situation.

As a response to this, the Corinthians began looking for ways to expand their own power and influence, and also to demonstrate to the Spartans just how annoyed they were at the terms of the deal they had reached with Athens.

They did this by appealing to Argos, a city-state that was located almost directly in between Corinth and Sparta (see map below) and that had also been a longtime adversary of Sparta. In fact, despite lying so close to Sparta geographically, Argos was not a member of the Peloponnesian League, and it was constantly looking for allies in a potential fight against Sparta, its most powerful and most dangerous neighbor.

This alliance between Corinth, their biggest rival within the Peloponnesian League, and a powerful city-state outside of the League would have significantly threatened Sparta's control over the League, which it needed in order to maintain its own autonomy, as well as defend itself from a pesky Athens that continued to try and expand. But Corinth was unwilling to directly defy Sparta, so it began supporting an armament effort in Argos, hoping this could cloak Corinthian support for a longtime Spartan rival.

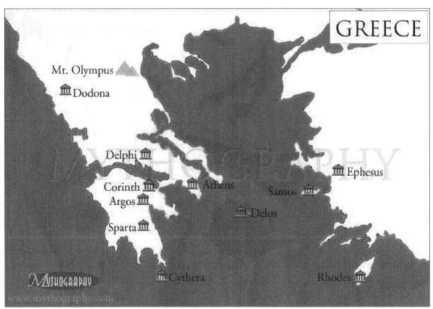

To make things even more troubling for the Spartans, several other states in addition to Corinth within the Peloponnesian League began to offer their support for Argos, specifically Elis and Mantineia. But to complicate things further, the Argives, those who come from

Argos, decided to renew their "nonaggression" treaty with Sparta while simultaneously agreeing to a defensive alliance with Athens, who was under the leadership of Alcibiades, a member of a prominent family with diplomatic ties to Sparta. This would have effectively ended the alliance Argos was negotiating with Corinth, largely because Corinth would never engage in an alliance with Athens, and although angry with Sparta, they recognized the need to stay in the Peloponnesian League. Additionally, this alliance between Argos and Athens also included Elis and Mantineia, putting the four of them on the same side against Sparta and the Peloponnesian League.

There is no real reason for any of this to occur other than the long-held bad blood between Sparta and Argos. However, one could argue that Argos was pushed into action by the Corinthians, who were seeking to annoy the Spartans after the Peace of Nicias. But no matter the reason, Sparta now found itself in a very precarious situation. Nearly all its enemies in the region had managed to come together, and even though the Peace of Nicias was supposed to last fifty years, it did not look as though Athens and Sparta would come close to reaching this target.

Not surprisingly, the result of all of this conspiring against Sparta was, as one might expect, a battle. Sparta brought together a large army made up of around 9,000 hoplites and brought it to Mantineia. They even appealed to their northern allies, such as Corinth, although they were unable to arrive in time. Thucydides would describe this force as one of the greatest ever assembled in the Greek world. And this force managed to win a decisive battle at Mantineia in 418 BCE that helped stop Argive aggression against Sparta and all but end the Argive/Athenian alliance. However, Athens' decision to align with and fight next to one of Sparta's most bitter enemies demonstrated just how unlikely it was that the Peace of Nicias would stand. Yet it would still be a little more time before the fighting would resume at full scale.

Athens Teams up with Melos

An underlying theme in the Peloponnesian War is that Athens was incapable of just letting things be. After their success against Persia and as the leader of the Delian League, they became an empire, and empires seek to expand. Yet this was extremely difficult for them to do, largely because of the presence of their powerful neighbors, the Spartans.

However, just because it was difficult didn't mean Athens wasn't going to continue to try. So, after their alliance with Argos failed, Athens began looking elsewhere for opportunities to expand their influence, but this time they tried to go after areas that were not aligned with or against Sparta nor itself, perhaps as an attempt to try and keep the peace.

A good target for this was Melos, an island state that had once been a Spartan colony but that no longer had allegiances to its old imperial master. Nicias had spent time campaigning there, but he had failed to bring Melos under Athenian control, and many Athenians saw this as a dark stain on their power in the region for Melos was small and relatively weak, yet the Athenians had failed to bring them under the umbrella of their empire or league of allies. The map below shows where Melos is in relation to Athens, and this helps show why the Athenians may have been interested in taking it. And because it was not aligned to Sparta, this would have been a good way to expand

Athenian power without provoking further trouble with the Spartans, or so they thought.

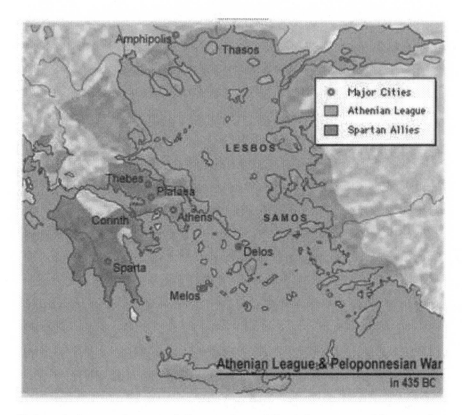

Athenian League & Peloponnesian War
in 435 BC

Using their superior naval fleet and wealth, Athens was able to rather quickly and easily bring Melos under its control. And while this didn't directly affect the relations between Athens and Sparta, it had an indirect effect that would most certainly help propel the two superpowers toward renewed conflict.

Most specifically, it emboldened Athenian leaders to continue campaigning in the name of conquest. Many historians use the speeches prepared by Thucydides for the leaders of Athens and Melos as a way of understanding how power and democracy were understood in ancient Greece, specifically how the Athenians saw expanding their power as the only way to expand democracy, something we would see in Napoleonic France more than two millennia later. As a result, many historians see this invasion and successful conquest of Melos the impetus for the next move by the Athenians: the expedition to Western Greece and the invasion of

Sicily. And this event most certainly provoked tensions between the Athenians and the Spartans which would lead to renewed fighting and the continuation of the Peloponnesian War.

The Athenian Invasion of Sicily

After success in Melos, the Athenians began to debate the possibility of sailing to Sicily to bring all the Greek states on the island under their control. A furious debate took place within the Athenian assembly. On one side, Alcibiades, the one responsible for the alliance between Athens and Argos, argued in favor of the expedition. And on the other side, Nicias, the moderate who had brokered the Peace of Nicias, was adamantly opposed to this mission of conquest.

However, in the end, Nicias lost, and it's likely this happened because of the Athenian connection of power and democracy with conquest. This had caused many people within Athens to become obsessed with the idea of expanding Athenian influence, and so it was therefore easy for leaders to obtain support for such initiatives.

Part of the reason Alcibiades was able to convince the Athenian assembly to approve this mission was because the Athenians had been told there were allies and money waiting for them on Sicily. The argument was that the most powerful city-state in Sicily, Syracuse, was disorganized and not powerful, and this left them ripe for conquest. So, in 415 BCE, the Athenians sent out a massive force that was made up of over 100 ships and thousands of men, commanded jointly by Alcibiades and Nicias, with support from Lamachus, a veteran soldier who was regarded as one of the more skilled military minds in the Greek army at the time.

But when the Athenians arrived on Sicily, they found out that the support that had been promised to them was not there, and the debate that ensued would have a huge impact on Athenian fortune there in Sicily.

Each commander had a different perspective. Nicias, who had been opposed to the expedition since the beginning, suggested they go around the island in search of allies and then return home if they didn't find any. But Alcibiades felt this was an unacceptable admission of defeat, largely since they had just found out the allies they had were actually false friends and he argued for trying to drum up support from local non-aligned Greeks and native Sicilians before launching an attack on Syracuse. And lastly, Lamachus argued that they should just take the force they had and launch an attack on the city. Syracuse was disorganized and therefore not well-defended, and the Greek soldiers were in high spirits and ready for battle. Most historians agree this strategy would have put the Athenians in the best position for success, but in the end, they chose Alcibiades' strategy.

This proved to be a fatal decision, for in the time spent trying to gather support from the locals, the Syracusans were able to organize themselves and set up a better defense. And to make matters worse, the Athenians failed to add to their ranks in the time they spent appealing to the locals.

Then, word came from Athens summoning Alcibiades to face trial for some religious vandalism that he had become connected with, but instead of returning home to be convicted for a crime and persecuted, he instead fled to Sparta and told them of the Athenians' plans on Sicily. This all but set the wheels of war in motion, as the Spartans responded by sending a small but effective force to help the Syracusans defend their city. The Corinthians also supplied ships.

The first bout of fighting led to Lamachus' death, and Nicias immediately sent word to Athens to be relieved. This request was denied, but the Athenian assembly did send more help in the form of Demosthenes, one of the generals who was responsible for the victory at Sphacteria. After he arrived, the Athenians attempted to lay siege to Syracuse by building a series of walls around the city. This became known as the Battle of the Walls which the Syracusans won decisively. Then, in an attempt to salvage the battle, the

Athenians decided to engage the Syracusans in a naval battle, but after having been fortified by the Corinthians, the Syracusans were able to beat back the Athenians. Nicias and Demosthenes then ordered a retreat which ended in not only their deaths but also the complete destruction of their entire army by 413 BCE. For all intents and purposes, the expedition to Syracuse had ended as a complete and total failure.

Conclusion

This middle period of the Peloponnesian War which took place between 421 BCE and 413 BCE did not see much direct conflict between the Athenians and the Spartans. But it did prove to be an important part of the overall conflict between the two powerful Greek city-states.

Overall, these years demonstrated a few important things. 1) The Athenian thirst for power had not diminished. As long as they were around, they were going to continue to try and expand their influence, and no matter what, this would always be a threat to Sparta. 2) The Athenians were all but incapable of beating the Spartans in a land battle. The best they could hope for was forcing a stalemate by using their powerful navy, but when the Corinthians got involved, this could level the playing field and force Athens into failure. And 3) the Peloponnesian League was proving to be much stronger than the Delian League. The Spartan armies combined with Corinthian fleets were proving to be a force that would be difficult to defeat in any battle.

As a result, this part of the war can also be considered a turning point. The Peace of Nicias marked the end of what was essentially a ten-year-long stalemate, but for the next eight years, the Spartans would grow stronger and the Athenians weaker, setting the conflict up for its final stage which would result in a victorious Sparta and an end to Athenian power in the ancient world.

Chapter 6 – The Ionian War and the Fall of Athens

The first ten years (431-421 BCE) of the Peloponnesian War are often called the Archidamian War, and the middle period (421 BCE-413 BCE) is sometimes referred to as the Interlude, mostly because this represented a break in the fighting that would set up the last round of conflicts, which is often referred to as the Ionian War, or sometimes the Decelean War. Some historians also call this period the "Drive to Decision," as the events that took place in the last nine years of the war would eventually produce a conclusion to a conflict that had been going on in one form or another for the entire 5ᵗʰ century BCE.

For those looking at this war with the perspective of a historian, it's easy to see how the handwriting was indeed on the wall for the Athenians. They had failed to win a decisive victory anywhere except Pylos, and even that was more luck than skill, and their attempts to expand westward into Sicily turned out to be a disastrous failure. And while they still held a stronghold in the Aegean Sea, which had long been their source of power, this would become the focal point of Sparta and the Peloponnesian League, which would eventually succeed in toppling Athenian power and ending their years of influence in the region.

Interestingly enough, the Spartans would receive help from the Persians, specifically the Achaemenid Empire, and this would be part of the reason why they finally were able to declare victory over the Athenians. But the fall of Athens also opened the door for the rise of the Macedonians who under the leadership of Alexander the Great would conquer all of Greece and Persia, dramatically reshaping the course of history in both Europe and Asia. But this was still a long way away, and the final nine years of the Peloponnesian War are some of the more interesting in all of Greek history, as well as the history of the ancient world.

The Beginning of the End for Athens

There is a story that in the fall of 412 BCE an Athenian commoner in the port of Piraeus was getting his haircut and began lamenting about the large-scale loss of Athenian life that took place in the far-off land of Sicily. It is then said that the barber immediately stopped and ran into Athens to deliver the news at city hall, thinking of course that he was the first person to hear of the defeat. However, it's unlikely that by 412 BCE the Athenian authorities had not already learned of the defeat in Sicily, but the story helps to show how shocking the defeat was, and the Athenian response to the defeat helps shed some light on their unwillingness to accept what had become essentially a certain defeat.

The Athenians likely learned of the defeat the summer before when the Spartans launched another attack of Attica, the region where Athens is located. But unlike other times where the Spartans attacked and then nearly immediately retreated, this time they established a permanent base in Decelea, which is part of the reason this last phase of the war is called the Decelean War. This move allowed the Spartans to engage in a new strategy. They could launch more frequent and further reaching attacks into the Athenian homeland, causing all sorts of damage and putting tremendous strain on the Athenian markets which were starting to come up short in supplying the people with what they needed for survival.

This advance by the Spartans into Attica combined with the defeat at Sicily demonstrated that there were some holes in Athenian power, and some of the stronger city-states throughout the territory traditionally held by Athens decided to seize this moment to exert their own independence. For example, Chios, an Aegean island state that had been a longtime ally of Athens and the Delian League, defected from the league, and Athens was powerless to stop this from happening.

However, this combination of events did not alter Athens' quest to maintain and even expand its power. The massive treasury in Athens which was located on the Acropolis held a large cash reserve, which in 412 BCE the Athenian government tapped into to begin building new ships for a new fleet, and they began recruiting people from all over the empire to man these ships and sail them into new lands where they would win glory for Athens. But this grand comeback would never really materialize. Small Athenian advances would be met with swift defeats, and before long Athens would fall and Sparta would become the sole Greek superpower.

Sparta Makes Moves on Athens' Aegean Empire

The Spartan decision to establish a base at Decelea in Attica was an important part of their strategy that would eventually bring Athens down, but as long as Athens held onto its dominance in the Aegean, it would be difficult for Sparta to be able to claim a decisive victory, as this was where most of Athens' wealth and power was derived.

Surprisingly, the person who is credited for championing both the strategy of establishing a permanent stronghold in Attica and also that of taking the Athenians out of the Aegean was Alcibiades. This is the name of the general responsible for alerting the Spartans of the

Athenian attack on Syracuse, and his name is scattered in the history of the events that led to the end of the war.

Eventually, Alcibiades would switch back over to support the Athenians, and despite his treacherous ways, he would be welcomed back as a hero, but only temporarily. However, before delving too much into the story of Alcibiades, it's important to take a look at how the Spartans carried out their strategy of trying to upset the Athenian stronghold of power in the Aegean Sea.

And fortunately for the Spartans, they would not be alone in this mission. The Syracusans, grateful for the help the Spartans and Corinthians had provided them during the Athenian attack, lent ships and troops for the campaign. Sparta also spent a good deal of time building up its own fleet, which it was able to do because of the funds provided by the Persian king, Darius II. Seeing that Athenian power was slipping, the Persians saw this as an opportunity to regain their stronghold in Ionia and the rest of Asia Minor.

However, this support alone would not be enough as long as the Athenians could still count on their many allies scattered throughout the Aegean, so it would be important for Sparta to upset these relationships if they hoped to have success in their effort to completely end the threat to their sovereignty that occurred as a result of a powerful Athens.

Fortunately for Sparta, things were starting to work in their favor. The decision to set up a permanent base in Decelea was paying significant dividends not only because it was putting stress on the Athenian markets, making her more and more dependent on overseas trade, but also the frequent Spartan raids from Decelea had put considerable stress on the Athenian silver mines, which meant that Athens was running out of money. To reverse this trend, it began to demand higher levels of tribute from its subject states and city-states, which only raised tensions within the empire and encouraged a more intense desire for rebellion.

So, to try and deliver the crushing blow to Athens, the Spartans began sending envoys into the Aegean to talk with those city-states who were becoming increasingly discontent with Athenian rule. The Spartans promised protection should these city-states rebel, and after some time, most of Ionia did indeed undertake a rebellion that put Athens into an extremely desperate situation.

But the Spartans were once again unable to secure a decisive victory. First, nearly all of Sparta's allies were slow to offer the support they had promised. This meant that Sparta was unable to offer some of the protections it had promised to states throughout the Aegean, and without the support of an Athenian enemy, these rebellious states stood little chance of winning, and therefore many of them decided to return to the Athenian side.

The other reason the Spartans were unable to deliver the crushing blow at this point in time was because they slightly underestimated the remaining strength of the Athenian fleet. After Syracuse, most believed that the Athenians had very few ships and soldiers left. And because Sparta, using Persian funds, was recruiting heavily and successfully throughout the Aegean, Athens' traditional source of manpower, they felt they had a massive advantage. However, this proved to not be the case. The Athenians had set up an emergency reserve consisting of ships and silver that was supposed to buy the Athenians enough time to fully rebuild their military. And in the beginning, it appeared this would be the case. The Athenians were able to defeat the newly-formed Spartan fleet at the Battle of Cynossema in 411 BCE.

However, this victory did not provide much of a tactical victory. Instead, its significance is derived from the timing around which it occurred. Specifically, the Athenian government had gone into shambles, and had its fleet been defeated, then this would have likely been the end of Athens. But a victory bought them some time to restore order on the home front, and this ended up giving them the opportunity to extend the war, which is another way of saying extending their independence.

Alcibiades and Unrest in Athens

Another impact of the massive Athenian defeat on Sicily is that it created a significant amount of discontent within Athens itself. First, it ruined Athenian finances, but it also caused people to lose faith in the Athenian democracy, an institution that had been in place for more than 100 years. And this lack of faith came from both the upper and lower classes. More specifically, the death of well-respected leaders, such as Cimon, Pericles, and Nicias, had left a hole at the top of Athenian government that were filled by less popular leaders, such as Cleon and Alcibiades, both of whom would damage Athenian chances at victory as a result of their blind ambition and hubris.

Because of this, some of the more powerful members of Athenian society, a group known as The Four Hundred, began conspiring to overthrow the Athenian democracy so that they could install an oligarchy, which means ruled by the few and was the main form of government throughout most of the Greek city-states over which Athens ruled.

However, interestingly enough, Alcibiades, who for some time had been working for the Spartans, began talking to members of The Four Hundred in Athens, and he encouraged the coup by telling the Athenian leaders that he had secured a guarantee from the Persians that they would change allegiances and support the Athenians if they were no longer ruled by a democracy.

Alcibiades could be found working for nearly all the parties involved. He had managed to convince the Persians that the best way to take down the Greeks was to support both the Athenians and the Spartans, but he was also helping the Spartans make moves against the Athenians, all while he was working to reestablish himself within the inner circles of Athenian government. Part of the reason Alcibiades was such a shapeshifter is that he does not seem to have been particularly well-liked by any of the people he was working with for most of his life. It's true he was welcomed back to Athens a hero, but this status was short-lived. Throughout his life, he had been condemned to death by the Athenians for religious vandalism, he had been accused of seducing the Spartan king's wife, and he was mistrusted by the Persians who saw him as a man only interested in his own self-interest.

But despite this mistrust from nearly all parties involved, Alcibiades managed to gain some support, and he used this support to actually win some victories for the Athenians, helping to stave off the Spartans for just a little bit longer. He did this by appealing to the people on Samos, which was an important city-state in the eastern Aegean (see map below).

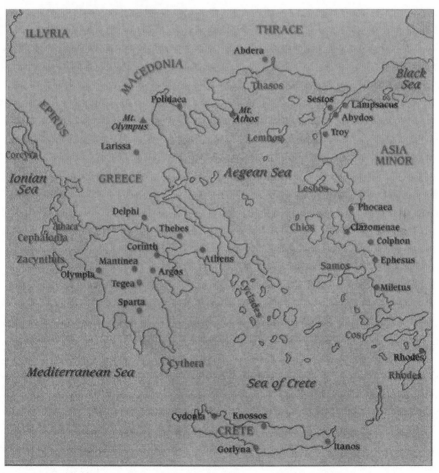

Samos is significant because it was another democracy within the Athenian Empire, and its leaders were also interested in overthrowing it in favor of an oligarchy. But the difference between Samos and Athens is that the Samian people were not as thrilled at the idea of relinquishing their entire democracy. However, because of where Samos is located, the Samians were actually able to call Alcibiades to come to Samos and speak to them about his plans and to elaborate on his supposed influence with the Persians.

Once in front of the Samians, Alcibiades told them the same thing he had told the leaders in Athens: the Persians would support the Athenians if they abandoned democracy and installed an oligarchy. But Thucydides reports that when Alcibiades spoke to those in Samos, a chance he didn't have in Athens, he actually subdued his language, suggesting that the Persians would support them if they no longer had a "direct democracy," which left the door open for democracy to remain intact, something that was a major point of contention in Samos at the time. This change made the appeal of Alcibiades seem more attractive because he was promising the support of the Persians, which the Samians and Athenians knew they needed in order to defeat the Spartans, but without forcing a complete overthrow of the democracy.

So, thanks to the combination of factors discussed above and to the scheming of Alcibiades, by 411 BCE the stage was set for a coup. In Athens, things went rather quickly, and on June 9, 411 BCE, The Four Hundred had managed to seize control of the Athenian government, effectively ending the Athenian democracy. However, things did not go quite as well in Samos where the appetite for a coup was different and where Alcibiades had made different promises. The primary military force at Samos, its naval fleet, resisted the attempts to overthrow the government and ended up deposing the conspirators and electing new ones. They also sent for Alcibiades to return to Samos and to be the commander of their fleet.

So, at this point in 411 BCE, Athens was in shambles. Samos declared it would continue the war against Sparta, but the newly-established oligarchy in Athens began to appeal to Sparta for peace. Shortly after taking power, they began construction of new fortifications of Piraeus, and it's believed that the plan was to hand this port over to the Spartans in peace negotiations. However, instability within The Four Hundred over how to deal with the Spartans created great problems for the Athenian rulers, and this eventually led to the installation of "the 5,000," which was an oligarchy that drew upon a much larger group of Athenian elites.

All of this unrest is the main reason why the Athenian victory at Cynossema became so important. Had the Athenians lost at the same time they were going through a coup and other political instability, it's more than possible that the Spartans would have been able to march into Athens and claim a decisive victory. However, this did not happen, and Athens was able to weather its own internal strife and come out in a much better position than that which they had been in since the invasion of Sicily and the attacks on Syracuse.

Alcibiades Leads an Athenian Comeback

In the end, though, the real winner in all of this is Alcibiades. After having been scorned by Athens just a few years earlier, he was now in command of a fleet, and he could use this to help him further increase his popularity throughout the Greek world. Alcibiades is an important figure in the Peloponnesian War, but he was clearly only looking out for himself. He schemed with many different competing interests to win himself back into favor with those who had hated him just a few years prior, and this meant that his position was always a precarious one.

However, this should not be taken as a discounting of his role in the final years of the Peloponnesian War. In fact, he came closer than the Athenians would ever come to victory again by winning the Battle of Cyzicus in 410 BCE. In this conflict, Alcibiades and his fleet routed the Spartans, destroying most of the ships they had sent to the naval battle and delivering a great victory for the Athenians. And in doing this, the Athenians had managed to regain control of much of the territory they had lost in the southern Aegean. But perhaps more significantly, this victory pushed the Spartans to sue for peace, but the Athenians rejected these overtures and continued onward with the war.

After the victory in 410 BCE, Alcibiades and his fleet sailed around the Aegean to engage the Spartans wherever necessary, winning several smaller yet still significant battles along the way. However, the Spartans had been badly beaten at Cyzicus, and they weren't able to keep up with the Athenians. So, by 407 BCE, Alcibiades returned to Athens, and when he got there, he was given a hero's welcome. And shortly afterward, he was elected to the prominent position of *strategos autokrator*, which was the highest rank in the Greek military.

However, as one might expect, Alcibiades had made many enemies during all the time he spent scheming and trying to make things work out in his favor. As a result, his time in power would come to an end rather quickly. He was sent off to command a campaign in Asia, but he was defeated, and his enemies conspired against him to have him killed. However, hearing of this plan, Alcibiades retreated into exile in Thrace, later moving to a province of the Persian Empire where he would live until 404 BCE, when an envoy of Spartans or Persians came and assassinated him.

Lysander Brings the War to an End

The Athenian victory in 410 BCE at Cyzicus and the subsequent years of Athenian success might paint the picture that the war was once again heading for a stalemate, even though the Athenians looked to be all but dead after their crushing defeat at Syracuse. However, the Athenians' rejection of peace after Cyzicus meant that war would continue, and in 406 BCE, Athens would once again win a major battle against the Spartan fleet at Arginusae.

But bad weather prevented the Athenian fleet from completely destroying the Spartans, and this led to a major trial in Athens that resulted in the execution of six top naval commanders. Many people in Athens felt this failure and the subsequent loss of property and life that occurred could have been avoided with better leadership and that those responsible for it should be punished, but this may have been just general frustration over what was probably seen as an imminent Spartan defeat. But in carrying out this punishment, the Athenians not only left the Spartans with the strength to continue fighting, but they also left themselves the task of continuing to wage war with a demoralized navy and without many top commanders.

This failure to finish off the Spartan fleet and the decision to eliminate such prominent leaders helped set the stage for Athenian defeat. Currently under siege from the Spartan forces located at Decelea, the Athenian population was facing heavy shortages in many staples. And because the Spartans had decimated most of the farmland in Attica, the Athenians relied solely on trade from the Dardanelles region of the Aegean, which is often called Hellespont, for its grains.

Recognizing this weakness, a Spartan admiral named Lysander decided it was time to switch the Spartan strategy from trying to take control of Athenian strongholds in the Aegean to instead increasing the burden of the siege being laid upon the city. Lysander has an interesting backstory because he was one of the first Spartan admirals to not be a direct descendant of the Spartan royal families. And because he had grown up in a time where the Spartans were focusing on their navy, he was a much more skilled naval commander than many of the commanders that had come before him.

Early in 405 BCE, Lysander led his fleet into the Dardanelles region, and because of its importance, what was left of the Athenian fleet had no choice but to follow. Lysander then turned around and launched a surprise attack on the Athenian fleet at Aegospotami, and this move helped deliver the decisive victory the war had been needing for some time. The Spartan fleet destroyed 168 Athenian ships and captured or killed some 4,000 Athenian sailors. Only twelve Athenian ships managed to get away, and this was essentially all that was left of the Athenian fleet.

So, with their fleet destroyed, their treasuries emptied, and their food supply completely shut off, Athens had no choice but to surrender, and they did so in 404 BCE. Those city-states that still remained loyal to Athens, such as Samos, also surrendered, although its people were allowed to flee with their lives. This capitulation meant that the Peloponnesian War had officially come to an end. And the Spartans, as victors, got to set the terms.

Corinth and Thebes, who had long been the subject of Athenian aggression, wanted the city to be destroyed and the people inside it to be enslaved. However, the Spartans rejected this stance on the grounds that the Athenians had contributed too much to the Greek people and culture to be completely wiped from the face of the earth. But to make sure the Athenians would never again cause trouble amongst the Greek people, they were stripped of their fleet, its walls were destroyed, and it was forced to give up all of its overseas protections. This represented a humiliating defeat, but after 27 years of war, the Spartans were likely keen to do all they could to ensure nothing like this would ever happen again.

Conclusion

This last part of the war, called the Decelean or Ionian War, is best understood as a prolonged inevitability. After the Athenians had been routed in Syracuse, it was clear their efforts to expand further were going to be futile. And this move also caused them to make several enemies who would later offer support to the Spartans in their attempts to crush the Athenians once and for all.

However, that Athens was able to last as long as it did after its defeat at Syracuse speaks to just how powerful it was at this point in time. It was able to recover rather quickly and put together a fleet that would stave off defeat for another nine years. But in the end, the Spartans had gotten better at managing a navy, and internal strife within Athens meant that their time had come.

After the war ended, the Spartan Empire began. They began collecting tribute from all of Athens' previous subject states, and they remained the most powerful Greek state for at least another half-century. But Sparta also pledged to protect Athens, stating that the two cities would share the same friends and enemies for the time to come. It's unclear how this would have been received in Athens after so many years of war, but the Athenians likely did not have much choice.

The Spartan victory helped usher in an era of peace in the Greek world. The Spartans installed an oligarchy in Athens, but soon thereafter, once things had settled down, democracy was restored. Athens came back onto the scene during the Corinthian War, which was fought between the Spartans and a combined force of Corinth, Thebes, Athens, and Argos, and this helped to restore some Athenian influence in Greek politics, as well as humble the Spartans. But in the end, all of this quarreling would end when Philip II of Macedon stormed in and conquered all of Greece, only to be assassinated with his newly-conquered lands turning over to his son, Alexander.

Nevertheless, it's important to understand the significance of this war in Greek politics. Athens and Sparta were always the most important city-states in the Greek world, and their war defined Greek history for nearly an entire century. And while Sparta won and proved its dominance, Athens will still go down in history as one of the greatest cities, and empires, to have ever existed on this Earth.

Chapter 7 – Fighting in an Ancient Greek Army

Although the Peloponnesian War is one of the most famous wars in all of ancient history, warfare at this point in time was not a particularly important part of Greek culture. In fact, the concept of a unified Greek army did not exist until the Greco-Persian Wars. Before this, each city-state was responsible for its own protection, and it wasn't until the threat of a large-scale Persian invasion that the Greeks banded together and formed what would nowadays be called an army.

However, after the Greco-Persian Wars, warfare became a central part of Greek life, largely because this conflict allowed both Athens and Sparta to gain considerable power which then put them in competition with one another. And as warfare became a more important part of ancient Greek life, the idea of training and holding a standing army became much more important, and this meant that the Greek city-states needed to improve not only how they trained their armies but also how they maintained and used them.

The Greek Hoplite

Far and away the strongest unit in the Greek army, the hoplite became a defining component of Greek warfare during the Peloponnesian War. The word hoplite derives from the word *hoplon*, which means an item of armor or equipment. Therefore, the word hoplite most likely means "armored man," or something similar.

What set hoplites apart from other units at the time was that they were extremely well protected. They carried heavy shields made of leather, wood, and bronze, and they wore protective clothing that was most likely made of animal hides. They also carried a *dory*, which was a spear that was somewhere between 6-9 feet long, although, in the armies of Alexander, most hoplites carried *sarissas*, which were 18 feet long. As a secondary weapon, hoplites would carry a *xiphos*, which was a short sword that was meant to be used when a soldier lost or broke their spear during combat.

However, the real strength of the hoplite came from its form of fighting. Hoplites would organize into a *phalanx*, which was a group of hoplites standing shoulder to shoulder. Typically, the first row of hoplites in the phalanx would stand with their shields out so as to protect themselves and those behind them, and the second row would extend out their spears so as to provide an additional level of defense to both the first and second rows of hoplites.

This type of fighting kept hoplites relatively safe as long as they didn't break rank, and it helped provide them with a significant advantage over less-protected armies, such as that of Persia. In fact, the Greco-Persian Wars was the first time hoplites engaged in battle with non-hoplites, and the success of the Greeks not only helped demonstrate their own effectiveness, but it also helped prove that the Persian army was not invincible, something that was a common belief at the time of the Greco-Persian Wars.

However, the hoplites were not without their weaknesses. Because they relied on the phalanx, hoplite formations were rather dependent on the bravery of the men standing in the front line. This is because enemies would usually engage a phalanx by running up to them and pushing. At this point, it was the responsibility of the second and third rows to push back. But should someone in the first row fall, or worse, get scared and try to run, then this would compromise this entire section of the phalanx.

Overall, the defensive strength of the hoplites and the phalanx contributed significantly to the Peloponnesian War; with both sides using hoplites, it became very difficult for either side to gain a real advantage, even though Sparta usually had larger, better-trained armies than their Athenian counterparts.

Additionally, at the beginning of the war, both sides were still using semi-professional soldiers. This means that armies would have to disband around the time of the harvest so that soldiers could return home and help out in the fields. However, in the final stages of the Peloponnesian War, when Sparta developed a strategy to finally crush their Athenian enemies, this practice was abandoned. The base the Spartans established at Decelea came with a change in policy about returning for harvest, which would have made it easier for the Spartans to launch raids into Attica and on Athens.

In general, serving as a hoplite was considered a great honor. The armor required to be a hoplite was very expensive, so it was often passed down from one generation to the next. Should a hoplite fall in battle, his fellow hoplites would do all they could to return the armor to the family so that it could either be sold as a way of supporting the family or so that the son could have it to carry on in his father's tradition.

Furthermore, in most Greek city-states, hoplites doubled as soldiers and citizens. They received some training, but their lives were split between being soldiers and whatever other profession they held. But in Sparta, there was a much stronger military tradition. Boys who were descendants of soldiers were often sent off to train much earlier than others, and they would have spent nearly their entire lives at war, making them professional soldiers, something that distinguished them from their adversaries. This is part of the reason the Spartans had such a significant advantage when engaging their Athenian counterparts, but it was often still not enough for them to gain that truly decisive victory that would end the war. To do this, the Spartans had to develop a navy that rivaled that of the Athenians.

Other Units in the Greek Armies

Besides the hoplite, the Greeks had lighter infantry, which was called the *psiloi*. These were part-time soldiers and part-time baggage carriers. They would have been from a lower class of Greek society, but they were important in battle. Most psiloi were javelin throwers, stone throwers, or slingers, and some were even archers, although this was rare. In fact, as war became more frequent in ancient Greece, the psiloi became more popular, largely because they were easier to replace but also because they could move around more easily than hoplites.

The other major non-hoplite unit that existed during the Peloponnesian War was cavalry. These units had been around for some time in Greek history, but outfitting cavalry units was often too expensive for Greek city-states. But in the Peloponnesian War, this changed, and cavalry became an important part of the Greek armies fighting in the conflict. They played every role they could play, which includes scouting, screening, harassing, outflanking, and pursuing.

Put together, the hoplites, the psiloi, and the cavalry made for a formidable force that was able to dominate ancient Greece. But since the Peloponnesian War consisted of Greeks fighting Greeks, it was difficult for either side to gain a significant advantage, causing high casualties.

Greek Naval Units

The Peloponnesian War was very much a naval battle. The Athenians derived most of their power from their Aegean strongholds, and because of their superior fleet, they had a significant advantage over the Spartans when it came to defending it.

In general, there were two parts of the Greek navy that made it strong. The first was the *trireme*, which referred to the type of ship used. The word trireme literally means "three rowers," and this was its defining characteristic. It was a galley with three banks of rowers on each side of the boat, one forward, one aft, and one in the middle, and this made it faster and more agile than other galleys at the time, something that provided the Greeks with a strong advantage against foreign enemies, and also the Athenians against the Spartans. A sketch of a Greek *trireme* is depicted below.

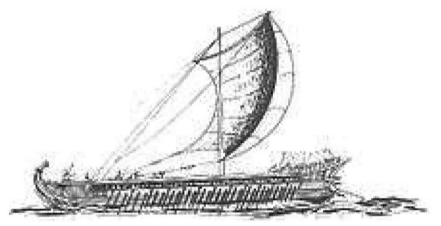

But part of the reason the Greek trireme was so effective was because of the way in which it was used. They had two main tactics, one being the *diekplous*, which had triremes attempt to sail in between enemy ships so that they could quickly turn around and attack and ram the back of the ships they were approaching. This tactic was highly successful before the Peloponnesian War, but it quickly fell out of style largely because opposing navies adjusted their strategy to defend against it.

The other main tactic that was used during the Peloponnesian War was the *periplous*, and this involved sailing around the enemy instead of through it so that, like the deikplous, the Greeks could attack their enemies from the rear. However, unlike the deikplous, the periplous proved to be rather effective, especially if the attacking triremes worked quickly, efficiently, and quietly.

To help the ships be more effective, each one was outfitted with marines and archers. These people were responsible for jumping onto and attacking enemy ships after they had been rammed. They were also the ship's main defense. It was their job to make sure those who were trying to board their own vessel were not able to do so.

Another tactic used frequently in Greek naval battles was shearing. The purpose of this attack was to ram a ship in its oars as this would cause them to splinter and slam back into the crew, maiming or killing them, and making it easier for the men on the attacking ship to jump aboard and capture and kill all the enemy sailors.

Conclusion

In general, Greek warfare was simplistic but effective. There was not much in terms of innovation throughout the Peloponnesian War, and the Spartans were those who improved the most. They started the conflict with a weak navy and a strong army, whereas the Athenians started with the opposite. And the Spartans were able to use their strong army to lay siege to Athens and other cities so that they could build up their navy and also gain enough allies to defeat the far superior Athenian fleet and eventually win the war.

Chapter 8 – The War's Impact on Greek Culture

When talking about ancient civilizations who have impacted the world in which we live today, it's hard to underestimate the role of the Greeks. Their advances in art, literature, philosophy, science, and technology are hard to beat in the ancient world. In fact, part of the reason we know anything at all about the ancient world is due to the Greeks.

As mentioned earlier, the great poet Homer started the tradition of recounting the events of the world with his epic poem *The Iliad*, even though much of what he told in this account may not have ever happened. But this tradition carried on with Herodotus, who was the one responsible for documenting the Greco-Persian Wars, and, of course, with Thucydides, who wrote down the world's first rigorous historical text about the Peloponnesian War.

But the Greek contributions to world culture are much bigger than this, and many of these great additions to history came as a result of the Peloponnesian War. Specifically, much of the art that came out of this time period reflects the attitudes about the war, bringing human emotion into art for perhaps the first time. Also, Greek philosophy, which would go on to influence many of the philosophical schools throughout history, took a great step forward with men such as Plato, Socrates, and Aristotle, all of whom were deeply affected by the Peloponnesian War.

And when we stop to think about it, this makes sense. The events of the world tend to impact the way people think about it, and the Peloponnesian War in many ways was the most important event to occur in the ancient Greek world. It pitted the two great superpowers against one another, and the damage caused by this conflict affected nearly every corner of Greek civilization and beyond. And this helped change the course of history and shape the world in which we live today.

Art During the Peloponnesian War

The art that was being made at this point in Greek history is in many ways a reflection of the intellectual climate that was going on in Greece around the outbreak of the war. Specifically, the Greeks were developing a keen sense of rationalism, meaning there was an increasing desire to understand reality for what it was and to explain it using logic and evidence to support that logic. This is part of the reason why Thucydides ended up writing the historical account that he did about the war: he was concerned with figuring out how to explain it in ways that didn't depend on the gods being angry or bad omens coming from the cosmos.

This approach to art is what helped develop what is known as "Classical" style, which is what would go on to influence much of the art that would come out of Europe later on in history. In fact, the Renaissance, which is responsible for producing so many of the world's most well-known artists and masterpieces, was based on this style.

But this classical style had been brewing in Greece for some time, and it can't be attributed entirely to the outbreak and heartbreak of war. However, the Peloponnesian War certainly did have an impact on how this classical style morphed throughout this period, yet it doesn't change it in the way we might expect. Unlike more modern art, where war made it much darker and more morbid, such as with Picasso's *Guernica*, the Peloponnesian War made art much softer and almost prettier. Some art historians argue this was a reflection of the escapism present in Greece at the time; with the land ravaged by war, plague, and political unrest, most Greek citizens were looking for a way to depart from their reality and deposit themselves in a different world. And for many, art was the way to do this.

Many of the sculptures that came out of this period were of naked women, and sculptors paid particular attention to the softness of the human form, making sure all the edges were as smooth as possible while making sure to not stray too far from how a body realistically looks.

However, this desire to use beauty and softness to escape from the harsh realities of war was not the only thing that defined Greek art at the time. Much attention was indeed paid to the anxiety and stress that came from living in a period where war was pretty much all the average person knew. And many of these examples can be found in the reliefs and sculptures that decorated the many temples that were built in ancient Greece. Temples still were considered to be the most important buildings in a city, and artists took this as an opportunity to depict some of the things people were thinking and feeling while war was waging around them.

A good example of this are the frieze reliefs that were sculpted at the temples in Bassai (modern Bassae), which are depicted below. These sculptures show men, women, and centaurs attacking each other in a ruthless manner, which is no doubt meant to reflect the violence of the age. Again, careful attention is paid to the human form, with the artists making sure to present it as realistically as they could while also paying attention to the supernatural, something that was still present in the minds of the ancient Greeks despite all of their rationalism.

These reliefs are often discussed in contrast to those that can be found at the Parthenon. Since these were created before the war, there is a feeling of togetherness in the Parthenon reliefs that is not felt in those at Bassai. The reason for this, according to art historians who have spent time studying the subject, is that the Bassai reliefs are meant to depict the chaotic nature of the age. The frenzied placement of the reliefs shows the haphazard nature of war, and it's also meant to symbolize the terror people must have felt and also some of the randomness of the violence that was occurring at the time.

This helps to put the war in a bit more context, or at least it helps us understand it in the way those living it would have. To the average Greek citizen, the war would have felt endless and perhaps even unnecessary, something we saw after the first ten years of the war. The people had grown tired of it, and it was very much those in power who kept it going. Those who can look back and study it can see there was a more linear path of events playing out, but this would not have been the case to contemporary Greeks, and this was very much reflected in the art that came out of this period in history.

However, despite this heavy emphasis on death and the stress and anxiety caused by war, there was another theme that came out of this period: victory. People may not have really wanted war, but since they were involved with it, they at least wanted to win it. And a great example of this can be found at the Athena Nike temple, which was constructed in Athens sometime during the 420s BCE, right in the middle of the war with Sparta. Athena and Nike are both goddesses, with Nike being the goddess of victory.

It's believed that some of the scenes depicted on this relief are from the Greeks' victory over the Persians at Marathon and other important battles in the Greco-Persian Wars, but there are other scenes that clearly show Greeks fighting other Greeks, something that can be discerned thanks to the attention to detail Greek sculptors usually had. But in these sculptures, another thing is worth noting, specifically the connection the Greeks made to victory in war and victory in sexual pursuits.

For example, one of the scenes depict Nike bending down to adjust her sandal, and in doing so, her breasts, as well as the rest of her body, are clearly defined. This has been interpreted by scholars of Greek art to be a symbol of the close connection between war and sexuality. It's true that this is not necessarily a new theme in terms of ancient art, but it's interesting in this context because it helps to show some of the changes that occurred in Greek society as the war began. Here is a picture of this particular Nike:

Specifically, it was mentioned earlier that one of the longer-term causes of the war was that the Greek youths at the time were hungry for war. Many of them were too young to have been able to participate in the great campaigns against Persia, and as a result, they were interested in finding ways to go out and win themselves glory and honor which presumably would bring them sexual success when they returned. However, these reliefs were created during the initial parts of the war. Those that represent more anxiety and stress, such as those at Bassai, were made toward the end of the war, and this helps show how Greek attitudes about the war had changed considerably over the course of the conflict.

However, with Greeks fighting Greeks during the entirety of the Peloponnesian War, artists were also forced to face the harsh reality of death, and in this, they once again decided to go for a romantic approach. A great example of this is the *Dying Niobid*, who was a goddess that proclaimed her children to be more beautiful than all the children of all the gods. But in exchange for this exaltation, the gods killed all seven of her sons and all seven of her daughters, and then they killed her. But as she was dying, she reached back to grab an arrow so that she could continue to fight, an allusion to the glory and beauty of dying for something that's important.

This particular sculpture, which was crafted in the midst of the war, captures nearly all of these thematic elements, and for this reason, it's considered to be one of the more important pieces of art to come out of this period. It is currently held in the National Roman Museum in Rome, Italy.

All of these elements combined to form a style of art which is known as the "Rich Style," and it is unique to this period in Greek history.

But sculpture wasn't the only art form that adopted this style during the war years. Paintings also depicted the sorrow and glory of war and the juxtaposition between life and death that many of these sculptures aimed to capture, and this can be used as further proof that the Greeks were experiencing this war not as some grand attempt to secure eternal glory but rather as a tragedy, something rather unique in ancient civilizations. Up until this point in time, the art surrounding war was mostly used as a way of glorifying the kings and gods responsible for it, and in turn, as a form of propaganda for securing the support of the people for constant warfare.

A good example of these is the white ground *lekythos*, which means "oil flask." These were drinking vessels, and they were often painted and decorated, making them some of the only remaining pieces of Greek paintings left. The lekythos depicted below shows a funeral ritual, and while it's sad, it doesn't depict death as some great tragedy but rather a certain truth we must all deal with. And this is certainly reflective of the style of the time and also of the escapism themes we see in other pieces of ancient Greek art.

These are important because these are what average people, more specifically women, would have been using in their homes, and this reflects an overall change in the way Greeks viewed death. With disease and starvation also killing off thousands, people began viewing death less tragically. Instead, they began to look at it more as simply a part of life, and this helps give a snapshot of what living in Greece would have been like at the time.

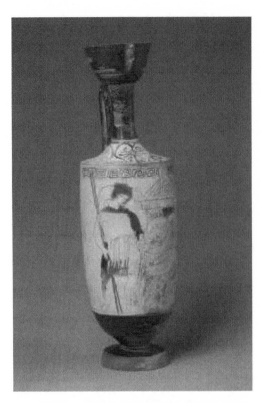

Literature from the Peloponnesian War

Literature is similar to art in that it helps tell the stories of the times. It's a good way for people who did not live during a certain period to understand what people were thinking, feeling, and discussing at a particular moment in history. And in ancient Greece, when we talk about literature, we end up talking almost exclusively about playwrights.

This is because plays were one of the principal forms of entertainment in ancient Greece, and most playwrights used plays as a way to make comments about what was going on in society at the time. As a result, it shouldn't come as much of a surprise that Greek literature at the time was heavily influenced by the events of the Peloponnesian War, as this was what was dominating the lives of nearly everyone living at the time.

However, the literature that comes from this period of time was a bit different from the art as it made little to no attempt to glorify the death and destruction that came from war. Instead, the plays that were written and performed at the time, specifically those that came from the famous playwright Aristophanes, deals with the concept of war weariness in a way that it hadn't been dealt with before.

The first of Aristophanes' famous plays to come out of the Peloponnesian War era was *Acharnians*, which was performed for the first time in 425 BCE, just six years after the outbreak of the war.

It is set in Athens, and its main character is an Athenian citizen who decides to seek a private truce with the Spartans, hoping this would help end the misery that had come to define his life. The reason he titled the play *Acharnians* was because this was a group of people living in the fields of Attica that had been considerably impacted by the repeated raids of the Spartans and their armies.

Aristophanes spends most of the play ridiculing the causes of the war, calling them trite and meaningless, and the play ends with the main character winning at a drinking contest which is meant to show that the end of the war, when it does come, will likely be as arbitrary as its beginning.

This particular play is certainly powerful in that it deals with the attitudes of many of the Greeks living at the time, but some of his other plays were even more poignant. For example, *Birds*, which was first performed in 414 BCE, is right around the time the Athenian expedition to Sicily was being revealed as a tremendous defeat.

This play, which features two main characters, Euelpides (hopeful son) and Pisthetaerus (persuading friend), is briefly set in Athens, but soon after the play begins, the two main characters decide to abandon Greece and fly off into space to establish a new civilization away from all the war. Then, once they are in their newfound land, they begin to construct a society that excludes everything they consider to be responsible for the war, such as oracle sellers and sycophants. Aristophanes also spends time discussing other things, such as war orphans and domestic instability, helping to reflect the overall state of discontentment people felt as a result of this long, drawn-out war.

The third play to come out of this era that's worth mentioning is *Lysistrata*, which was released to the public in 411. In this piece, the women of Greece decide to go on a sex strike so as to bring the war to a close. This represents a big shift in perspective as it shows the Greeks willing to allow the Persians, who are supposed to be the enemies of all Greeks, the upper hand in the conflict, something that just fifty years before would have been completely inconceivable.

The other major playwright of the time, Euripides, dealt with similar topics as Aristophanes, but he did so in a decidedly different way. His three main works that came out during the Peloponnesian War, *Andromache* (c. 430-424 BCE), *Hecuba* (425/4 BCE), and *Trojan Women* (416 BCE), all feature women as their protagonists, which should be taken as rather strange for a society in which men dominated. And all of these plays have Trojan themes, meaning they are set in Troy.

In general, it's believed Euripides did this so that he could make bolder statements about the horror, cruelty, and wastefulness of war. However, his plays are also a good depiction of overall Greek attitude toward war. His first work, *Andromache*, talks about the Spartans as being evil instigators who were responsible for starting the war, which would have been a popular thought among many Greek citizens at the time. However, as time goes on, he abandons this idea that there is indeed one aggressor and switches instead to focus on the pure harshness that living with war can bring.

Other plays that he wrote, such as *Helen* (412 BCE), are more explicit in admonishing war. In this play, Euripides takes a different approach to the long-told story of Helen of Troy. For those who don't know, this is the story behind the famous Trojan War; the prince of Troy, Paris, apparently stole Helen of Sparta for his own, and this caused the Spartans to wage war on the Trojans until this great city was left in ruins. However, in Euripides' play, Helen turns out to be in Egypt. She was taken away to safety by spirits, and the point of this play is to clearly show that most wars fail to do what they say they will, and the death and destruction they produce is nearly always a tremendous waste.

Conclusion

Overall, the art and literature that came out of the Peloponnesian War all centers around one common theme: the Greek people were sick of war. This makes sense. The conflict we call the Peloponnesian War lasted 27 years, but Athens and Sparta had been fighting each other for nearly fifty years. But knowing what we know about the Athenian leadership at the time—that it desired to expand its empire and its power—it also makes sense that this public sentiment was all but ignored by those in positions of authority.

But this aversion to war should be taken as an interesting step forward in human culture. Nowadays, we know the toll war can take on people, and generally speaking, governments of today try to avoid war whenever they can. However, this was not a common line of thinking in the ancient world. In fact, war was often seen as something desirable, something we can see by the way the Greek youth approached the possibility of a great war between Athens and Sparta. But the sheer scale of the Peloponnesian War seems to have changed this perspective to one that was more aware of the consequences of war. And this can be seen as just another contribution the Greeks made to the world's understanding of morality and ethics, something that continues to shape the world even up until the present day.

It's interesting to note, though, that most of this culture that comes out of the Peloponnesian War is Athenian. It's not that the Spartans were not thinking of these issues but rather that their culture did not support the type of expression that the Athenians did. It's likely for this reason that Sparta chose to spare Athens after it had finally won the war. It knew that Athens was an invaluable part of Greek history, and it was therefore unwilling to destroy the city and permanently remove one of the key drivers of Greek culture.

Chapter 9 – Philosophy During War: Socrates

Any discussion about Greek history must pay some attention to philosophy, arguably the greatest contribution the Greeks ever made to world history and culture. The questions raised by the famous Greek philosophers such as Plato, Pythagoras, Epicurus, Democritus, and, of course, Aristotle and Socrates, and the answers they provided to these questions, are still relevant today and are in many ways still being discussed.

However, by the time of the Peloponnesian War, the Greek philosophical tradition was already well developed, and in fact, many of the philosophers mentioned above lived long before the war ever broke out. However, Plato, who was said to be Socrates' student, and Aristotle, who was Plato's student and also Alexander the Great's teacher, came right before and right after the war, coincidentally leaving Socrates as the leading philosophical thinker of the time.

Because of this, Socrates both influenced and was influenced by the war, and his writings and teachings based on this lived experience would go on to have a great impact on the collective Greek psyche and also on the way many of the leaders at the time thought about the war, helping to shape events. And to understand just how influential Socrates was in this period, we need only to look at the fact that just five years after the war ended, in 399 BCE, he had been locked up in jail and sentenced to death for having disrupted the peace and for having "put ideas" in people's heads that the powers at be considered to be quite dangerous.

However, looking back on history, we can see that this move was just another example of authority trying to maintain its position by persecuting those who dared to question it, and this makes studying Socrates during this time period all that much more important.

Who Was Socrates?

According to Plato, Socrates' student, Socrates was 70 when he died, which meant he would have been born in 469 BCE. This was well before tensions between Athens and Sparta had escalated but not so much before that he wouldn't be around to watch them grow and eventually turn into war. And he would also have considerable firsthand experience with the war for he served as a hoplite during the Archidamian War. Specifically, he fought in the famous battles at Potidaea (432 BCE) and also Amphipolis (422 BCE), where he was noted for his bravery and valor.

However, after the Peace of Nicias (421 BCE), Socrates did not see much more battle action for he would have been too old and therefore disqualified for battle. But he continued to play an important part in the war, serving as part of the Athenian Council of 500 which was responsible for administering many of the day-to-day activities of Athens. It was around this time that Socrates began to delve into issues of philosophy, and some of his ideas ended up getting him in trouble. In fact, it was part of what he did during his time as a member of this council that eventually led to his conviction for "corrupting the youth" of Athens as well as "worshiping false gods," and this inquisitive nature of his can be attributed to what made him such a great philosopher.

Specifically, when the naval generals who had failed to utterly destroy the Spartans at Arginusae and whose folly had caused significant loss of life and property were returned to Athens for trial, Socrates stood before an angry mob and argued that condemning these men to death for their error was illegal and would not be permitted. However, his argument fell on deaf ears, and the council eventually voted to indeed execute these commanders.

Something similar happened shortly after the Spartans had forced the Athenians to surrender. Hoping to get rid of Athens' "troublesome" democracy, the Spartans installed an oligarchic regime that came to be known as the Thirty Tyrants. This group installed a reign of terror that was designed to subdue the Athenians and prevent further unrest. But among these thirty were relatives of Plato, and these relatives, in an effort to expand the power of this small group of people, ordered Socrates to arrest a man who was considered an "illegal alien" and seize all of his property. But he refused, and the man was eventually arrested and killed anyway. But to the public, Socrates had been a conspirator, and this was in part the reason why he was later put on trial and eventually sentenced to death.

Socrates' Morality

The takeaway from these events is something that would come to define Socrates not only as a philosopher but also as a person. He became a great champion of ethics and morality, arguing that people must always do what is right. At one point, he argued that the citizens of Athens and of Greece in general needed to spend more time taking care of their souls, or in other words, they needed to concern themselves more with doing the right thing.

It's likely this perspective was established based on what Socrates saw whilst living in Athens. The frequent warfare combined with devastating plague caused many of the citizens of Athens to adapt a "you only live once" mentality, meaning they began to abandon the rule of law and morality because they expected to be dead, either from battle or illness, before they would have to face any consequences for their actions.

Another example of Socrates doing the "right" thing even if it was not socially acceptable was his rejection of the idea that education and independent thought was something that only the state could administer. In fact, Socrates used to travel around and offer "classes" to people who willing to pay for it, and this was something that was simply not done at the time. But it was his belief that people should be able to access whatever type of education they wanted to, and therefore he didn't think it right that only the government was able to educate people. But he caught a lot of criticism for this belief, and this may have been another one of the reasons why he was eventually persecuted for his work.

As you can see, Socrates' morality got him in trouble, for it often flew in the face of what the authorities were demanding at the time. But it was also what helped shaped Greek philosophy of the time and turn it into a leading school of philosophical thought. This is because Socrates was one of the first philosophers to get people to stop thinking about things that were going on in the cosmos. Instead, he was far more interested in contemplating what was happening on Earth between people. He is credited with "bringing philosophy down from the sky," and this represented a major change in the way people approached the field of philosophy in ancient Greece.

This approach taken by Socrates can help explain some of the thinking at the time, especially some of those themes that appeared in Greek art and literature during this period in history, specifically the idea that war might be wrong. The people were clearly fed up with the idea of constant conflict after a while for they had to experience firsthand the horrors that it can cause. And when you combine this lived experience with the teachings of Socrates, as well as the Sophists (a group of philosophers who existed around the same time and who also dealt with issues of morality), it becomes easier to see why war would have become so unpopular so quickly.

But beyond just his emphasis on doing the right thing, Socrates and his fellow philosophers helped to shape public opinion about the war with their ideas that people should look to take care of themselves before dedicating themselves too much to what's going on in the heavens. This idea would have caused people to doubt the type of unquestioned support for war that was previously the norm in the ancient world. Before this time, and afterward in many other cultures, war was understood as a part of destiny. It was something willed by the gods, and this made it the responsibility of the people.

However, the growing rationalist sentiment in ancient Greece, which started before Socrates entered the scene and expanded after he began to speak more publicly, would have rejected this idea that war was necessary. Instead, the people would have been more capable and willing to question the notion of war and to wonder if it was indeed the "right" thing to do. And after several decades of conflict and plague, with little or no success, the majority of people began to see war as not only wasteful but unnecessary.

Now, this idea can certainly be debated. Throughout history, there have certainly been times when war was completely and entirely necessary, but for the Greeks living during the Peloponnesian War, which was the largest and bloodiest in Greek history, this would have been a hard truth to swallow, and for the first time in history, people were equipped to articulate this doubt, contributing to a strong feeling of war weariness that ended up having a significant impact on the people living at the time.

However, somewhat surprisingly, one other impact Socrates had was that he was not a supporter of democracy. This may come as a shock to some for modern thinking dictates that democracy is always better and the "right" thing to do. But for Socrates, he saw governing as a job just like any other, and he felt that the only ones fit to do it were those who had received special training in the field and who had spent time training and practicing to be effective leaders.

He brought up the idea that sick people go to doctors because they are considered to be experts in understanding and curing disease, and that this was the same thing as governing. It does not make sense to ask someone who has no idea how to run a city's finances or deal with foreign diplomats to serve as the governor of a *polis* (city). But this idea was not particularly popular, and it's believed that Socrates' support of it is one of the reasons why he eventually faced persecution for his ideas. The idea of democracy was sacred in ancient Greece and anyone who questioned it was probably a tyrant, even if all they were doing was employing logic to make a point.

Conclusion

Rationalism and morality were two key ideas that were promoted by Socrates and had a strong effect on life in Greece during the time of the Peloponnesian War. They pushed people to think more than they ever had before about the causes of war, and perhaps more importantly, they encouraged people to question if war was necessary and right.

Of course, students of history can look back and say probably not, but at the time, this was not as obvious. In fact, during the early parts of the war, most people probably did see it as necessary. But the advanced understanding of public life that Socrates and his followers pushed through helped to change this perspective, which eventually contributed to significant war weariness and a loss of support of the war. However, this would not end up having much impact on the outcome of the war, as the authorities pushed forward with the war despite a lack of public support, suggesting that democracy in Greece may not have been as strong as many like to think it was.

Conclusion

Looking back with a historical perspective, one could easily say the outbreak and the outcome of the Peloponnesian War were both inevitable. After the Greco-Persian Wars, Sparta and Athens had both become extremely powerful, and their competing interests meant that they would soon be forced to fight for supremacy in the Greek world. An ambitious Athens could never exist alongside the more conservative and inward-looking Sparta which would see every attempt to expand Athenian influence as a threat to Spartan sovereignty.

However, its inevitability does not make it any less significant. The ancient Greeks were tremendously influential in shaping the world that we now live in today, and the Peloponnesian War played a huge part in making this happen. It reduced the power of Athens and set the stage for the first Spartan Empire, but it also helped create the conditions needed for Macedon to take over which eventually led to the rise of Alexander the Great, arguably the greatest conqueror in history.

But the war's impacts were considerably more far-reaching. The conflict helped to reshape Greek politics, but it also sent Greek art, literature, and philosophy in an entirely new direction. It helped fuel classical styles, and it ushered in an age of rationalism that would continue until Rome fell and that would help to define the world in which we live today. Furthermore, the war gave poets such as Aristophanes and Euripides a muse that would allow them to create some of the world's best pieces of literature, and it would give Socrates, one of the most well-known philosophers of all time, something of real importance to analyze and contemplate.

Overall, the glorification of war in many ways helps to perpetuate it, but this idea is a modern one. In ancient times, war was a way of life. It was necessary to secure safety and survival, and in this case, it helped one of the most developed cultures of all time enrich itself and offer more to the world than it could have ever hoped to have.

Check out another book by Captivating History

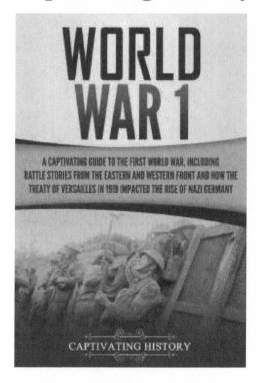

Bibliography

Bury, J. B, and Russell Meiggs. *A History of Greece to the Death of Alexander the Great*. London: Macmillan, 1956

Feetham, Richard, ed. *Thucydides' Peloponnesian War*. Vol. 1. Dent, 1903.

Kagan, Donald, and Bill Wallace. *The Peloponnesian War*. New York: Viking, 2003.

Pritchett, W. Kendrick. *The Greek State of War* The University of California Press, 1971

Sage, Michael. *Warfare in Ancient Greece: A Sourcebook*. Routledge, 2003

Tritle, Lawrence A. *A New History of the Peloponnesian War*. John Wiley & Sons, 2009.

26597968R00068

Made in the USA
San Bernardino, CA
20 February 2019